# Northeast Trout, Salmon, and Steelhead Streams

*Every River has a Story*

John B. Mordock

D0993014

*Frank*
**A mato**
PORTLAND

In memory of Robert Young

*In dreams the links of life are united;*
*we forget that our friends are dead;*
*we know them as of old.*

—Henry David Thoreau

Frank Amato Publications, Inc.
P.O. Box 82112, Portland, Oregon 97282
503.653.8108 • www.amatobooks.com

All photographs by the author unless otherwise noted.
Illustrations: Dürten Kampmann
Book & Cover Design: Kathy Johnson
Printed in Singapore
Softbound ISBN: 1-57188-311-8 • UPC: 081127-00145-3
1 3 5 7 9 10 8 6 4 2

# Contents

# CHAPTER ONE

# Putting It Into Perspective

Some anglers seek freestone rivers while others seek spring creeks. For others, perfection is not the river itself, but a perfect moment on it—the fly well cast, the fish well fought, the sunset beheld, or a stirring experience shared. Although perfection may seem important, the memory of it is what we hold dear.

This book is about my memories—memories of fishing wonderful rivers and having perfect moments on them, memories of the people who fished with me, and perhaps, most important, memories of those who took substance from the rivers and of those who gave substance back. Perhaps, the great African-American poet, Langston Hughes put it best when he wrote:

I've known rivers:
I've known rivers ancient as the world
and older than the flow of human blood in human veins.
My soul has grown deep like the rivers.

I've known rivers:
Ancient dusky rivers.
My soul has grown deep like the rivers.

Throughout history stories have been told, not just to pass on the wisdom of the storyteller—that would be presumptuous—but to nourish the minds and spirits of those listening. A story can touch common cords of hope, delight, and torment. In the simple act of telling a story a seed is planted, a seed that may grow and last a lifetime.

Some of the stories I will tell were based on my experiences, others on experiences shared with me, and still others on the experiences of those who came long before me, experiences that sparked my enthusiasm to fish a specific river. I hope the stories will allow readers to get a mental picture of each river, because with meaningful imagery a visit to a river can be more meaningful. Perhaps my stories will release readers from troubled minds and transport them to far off places, enlarging their personal geographies and their sense of possibilities.

Because rivers are always on the move, they are never the same. Richard Moe, president of the National Trust for Historic Preservation, once remarked: "More and more people are seeing that every place in America looks like every place else, and that means every place looks like no place." Most of us fish rivers to escape from such monotony. We seek special places that we can borrow for a short time. And each of these special places has some unique story waiting to be told about it, a story that stimulates the imagination, enlightens the mind, or captures the heart. Unlike the River Lethe, the river of forgetfulness where no lesson takes hold, America's rivers were first ridden by people hoping for new possibilities around the next bend, profiting from what they learned along the way.

For readers who have fished the rivers I describe, this book will provide an opportunity to compare notes, chuckle at the humbling episodes, or enjoy light reading between hatches. The stories I tell about my own adventures on each river are probably similar to ones other visitors might tell, enabling readers to relate my exploits to their own experiences. Perhaps, my stories will rekindle memories and create a craving for lost experiences

But the stories about the people who drew life from each river is another matter. Many anglers may not know them. I didn't know some of them when I first fished each of the rivers. Had I known them at the time, my angling experiences would have been enriched. The chief purpose of sharing these stories, therefore, is to help readers appreciate what each of these uniquely different rivers has to offer. (In any case, I will pass on what each river taught me.)

## What I Have Learned

Much of what I learned about each river I learned from other fishermen. I have never met a fisherman who didn't like to swap stories with me. Anglers, unlike members of some groups, often solicit the opinions of others, but rarely try to overwhelm others with theirs. By and large, we are a humble group, as fishing is humbling, as well as gratifying. This book might make some readers better fishermen, but only if they benefit from the experiences I share. The book makes no conscious effort to be instructional. Too many instructional books already exist on fly-fishing.

An English poet once wrote. "Opinion in good men is but knowledge in the making," and my Uncle, Jim Adams, who taught me to fly-fish, said, "Stay in conversation with the world—you both will be enriched."

Writers of instructional books should pay heed to the "The Four Wise People," an ancient story recently retold by Gail Neary Herman. I will quote the beginning of the story.

Once there were four wise people who lived a long time ago in a faraway place in India.

Three of them read everything they found. They never talked to anyone. They never asked questions. They just read, morning noon and night. They didn't put their books away until it was time to go to sleep.

But the fourth wise person often left late in the afternoon to walk and talk among the people. There was so much to learn from them. The fourth wise person would ask "How do you make your garden grow so big?" For they knew the secrets of agriculture. "How do you keep your livestock so healthy?" These were the secrets of husbandry.

The other three wise people just laughed to think anyone would waste precious time in talking and asking questions.

The story goes on to tell that the three wise persons, who never talked to people, needed a test for their knowledge. The forth wise person accompanied them on their journey to find this test. Eventually, they came upon a pile of bones. The first wise person decided to reshape the bones into the skeleton of the animal it once was. When he was done, the second wise person recognized the shape from his readings as that of a tiger. He decided to transform the skeleton with fur to make it look exactly like the tiger it once was. Looking at the inert structure, the third convinced the others that, if they all worked together, they could breathe life back into the tiger. Promptly, they began, with their equipment and their chemicals, and, utilizing all their learned knowledge, to complete the task of breathing life back into the tiger.

The fourth wise person cautioned them, saying he didn't think it was a good idea to breathe life back into a tiger! The others disagreed, saying their accomplishment would be a great scientific and technological breakthrough. The forth wise men climbed a tree. With all three of them working feverishly, the tiger began to move its legs, to turn its head, and to breathe, and within seconds the three wise people were gone. After the tiger licked his chops and lumbered off, the fourth wise person climbed down from the tree.

Some experiences are matters of the heart and not of the brain. They can't be explained. For example, I have learned when I will catch nothing from certain rivers. When I arrive and examine the river, it often appears lifeless. It is not just the absence of swifts or swallows, darting to and fro, or of hatching flies, it's the total feeling the river gives me. (Intuition cannot be communicated!) I don't know how to describe a sleeping river, but Robert Traver, blessed with superior observational and descriptive skills, wrote the following in *Trout Madness*:

"On some days the surface of the water possesses a peculiar gunmetal sheen, a kind of bland, polished, and impersonal glitter, a most curious sort of budging look, coupled with the aloof, metallic quality and cold, glassy expression of a dowager staring down a peasant through her lorgnette. At the same time there is a deceitful appearance of warmth, an opaque expression of bland geniality, and the light reflects off the water in a curiously false friendly way. It is all very subtle and confusing and hard to describe, yet when I see it I never for an instant mistake it. On such days, fortunately rare, I have learned that I might just as well leave my rod in the case and instead go chase butterflies or lurking girl-scout leaders."

The poetic angler might proclaim that the water spirit has conveyed that the river is sleeping and is not to be disturbed. The ancients believed that each body of water has a water spirit all its own. The water spirit is a living part of every stream, watching over the water and caring for it like a guardian. The water spirit is usually invisible to human beings, but if it has learned that an angler is a friendly visitor, a fellow protector who values the river deeply in his or her heart, it may communicate the river's secrets. It may disclose that the river will give up no fish today and encourage the angler to save the effort and go home. Some mysteries about trout and their world should remain mysteries. Shakespeare wrote of "nature's infinite book of secrecy." Must we open all its pages?

Some outdoor writers act as if catching fish is of great importance. I once spotted my neighbor's boy fishing along the shoreline of the small bass lake on which I lived. He was using a safety pin instead of a hook, and the pin was attached to string that was attached to a stick. He declined my offer to replace his safety pin with a fish hook, or to loan him a spinning rod, stating that he really didn't care that much if he caught a fish as he was having fun just being by the lake. Perhaps he should write a book!

When I first went to each of these rivers, getting there was of utmost importance. Now I know that the "there" is a place in the heart. Native Americans call this new consciousness "walking in a sacred manner." Since the river Jordan, people have used rivers in their search for things. They have also used rivers as havens. Clear, free-flowing rivers bestow a sense of inner peace that is refueling. After I fish a river, I return home with renewed vigor, with new appreciation for my family and friends. Like many anglers, I now gain greater pleasure from the environment where I fish and from the experiences I have while fishing than

from the actual capture of fish.

Each of the rivers discussed has an environment that is well-worth experiencing. The real value in angling is not simply catching fish but becoming closer to Mother Nature and getting in touch with her natural rhythms. In her poem, "The Fish that Walked," Ann Sexton wrote that the fish announced, after it had risen from water to walk on land:

> Though it is curious here,
>    unusually awkward to walk.
> It is without grace.
> There is no rhythm
>    in this country of dirt.

I try to create a larger image than just the riverside environment—to place the river within a larger context. Hiking trails overlook many of the rivers I fish. I try to hike them all. Some rivers can be looked down on from a mountain road. Others can be seen from the tops of ski slopes. Standing on a mountain top and marveling at the view before me, I better appreciate the river's place in the greater scheme of things. And each time I fish the river, the image from the mountain top anchors my smaller river adventure in a much larger world.

## My Angling Companions

My wife, Melody, has been with me to most of the rivers discussed, but I fished them in the company of long-time angling companions Scott Daniels, Tom Royster, and Bob Young, with Mike Zelie becoming a companion in more recent years. Scott was the Commissioner of Solid Waste in Dutchess County, New York, but the guy who kept all our fishing junk organized was Bob, who recently died of heart failure. He used to work as a

*Bob Young stalking wary wild trout on Upper Roundout Creek.*

psychologist at the agency where I was an administrator and because he was an idealist, our professional relationship often interfered with our personal one, but it seldom interfered with our fishing together. Fishing was a place to free ourselves from such conflicts. Tom lives in a little house on the upper Wappinger Creek and all of us have fished by his house many times or napped in his creek-side hammock when no fish were feeding. I must say that none of us are alike and while we sometimes see something in each other that is odd, even outlandish, it is our diversity that makes us colorful. This same diversity is in nature, but nature never argues about who is best, it simply goes about its business of being different.

While I enjoy fishing alone, fishing with a friend provides opportunities for closeness unavailable in normal social interactions, such as holding onto each other while wading across a swift river, keeping branches from hitting one another when walking a trail, assisting each other after a stumble, dusting each other off after a fall, unhooking each other's flies from a tree, netting each other's fish, unhooking a fly from the skin, and, best of all, sharing laughter, the type that is deep and kind.

## Where Would You Go?

V. S. Hidy opens his photographic collection, *The Pleasures of Fly-fishing*, with a quote from Ben Hur Lampman:

> Where would you go? With the will and way of it, and never a care for time, nor a fret for absence, and all the eagerness, where would you go?

I expect that an angler traveling in the East would go to one of the major rivers I discuss in this book, although I will refer to other Eastern rivers as well. Those featured are the Ausable, Battenkill, Beaverkill, Neversink, Willowemoc, Delaware, Esopus, Housatonic, tributaries to the Moose Lake (landlocked salmon rivers), Salmon (a chinook, coho, and steelhead river), and several small Catskill streams. The rivers discussed are considered among the best rivers in the East, rivers steeped in tradition and popularized in outdoor literature. Consequently, they are the rivers out-of-state fishermen visit each year. For example, surveys taken by anglers on the Beaverkill reveal visitors from 40 states.

Throughout this book I stress the rewards of angling for wild rather than for stocked trout. I will discuss each river's population of fish and give my opinions about them. To remain good wild trout waters, some of the rivers featured are in need of major environmental efforts to restore them to their prime. The Battenkill, Schorarie, and Esopus may never be as good as they once were.

## Accommodations and Other Activities

Many anglers travel with family members who don't fish. Even if some do, like my wife and children, they have the patience to do so only for short periods. When they were younger, my daughters, Kalay and Kaylin, enjoyed rowing for me while I cast to fish in ponds, but they were only good for about an hour, not because their strength gave out but because they wanted to do something else. My sons, Marten and Massen, could only fly-fish for an hour or so, particularly when trout were rising all around us and we couldn't catch any! My wife, Melody, likes to read sitting on the riverbank, but she can't do so when it lightly rains (and I get out my blue-winged olives) or at dusk when the big ones begin to feed. Since many good trout streams are located in relatively isolated areas, bored or restless family members can spoil the experience for others. In each chapter, I will list places to stay, followed by a discussion of other recreational opportunities near each river that family members might enjoy.

# CHAPTER TWO

# The West Branch of the Ausable
## *A River with Many Faces*

For many years, I used to stop at Fran Better's fly shop in Wilmington, New York—the lone gathering place for Ausable River fishermen during the late 1960s and 1970s—to get the scoop on river conditions. The shop, near the base of Whiteface Mountain, called the Adirondack Sports Shop, was a landmark for anglers visiting this northern New York river, a river that begins high up on Mount Marcy, the same mountain that spawns the mighty Hudson River.

I was initially attracted to the Adirondacks by my childhood memories of James Fenimore Cooper's "Leather-Stocking Tales," based upon an old Cooperstown woodsman, named Shipman, who wore leather footgear. *The Last of the Mohicans* also took place in the Adirondacks and it was my favorite. After failing to bump into the famous woodsman, I realized that the West Branch more than made up for this disappointment.

Five miles of the West Branch were set aside in 1994 as catch-and-release water. These new regulations were instituted to stimulate the return of a healthy wild trout population and to create "the two- to four-pound brown trout that were so frequently caught in the 1960s," referred to by Lee Wulff as *average* fish. To insure that anglers will once again catch "two-pounders" the state stocks a number of 13- to 18-inch trout in the river, and occasionally stocks as many as 800 browns up to eight pounds from its brood stock, and the Wilmington Chamber of Commerce, stocks fish from two to four pounds.

## A Teaching River

Unlike other Eastern rivers which suffer from diminished insect life, predictable mayfly hatches occur—with the Hendrickson hatch the most out-standing. It is a river where the angler will be reminded that fly-fishing isn't about casting, it's about fishing. Ray Bergman spoke fondly of the river in his classic work *Trout*, writing that the river was a, "stream wildly fascinating, capable of giving you both a grand time and a miserable one."

I have minimized the miserable times by closely examining the water, walking the riverbank to look for feed-ing fish, and inspecting different types of water, either by foot or from my car. Sometimes, birds give me a clue. When they are circling about, a hatch is usual-ly in progress, about to begin, or close to ending in the section where they dart to and fro. Because the river differs from section to section, flies can be hatching in one section and not in another. When no flies are hatching, I work stone flies deep in the pocket-water.

In long slow pools, such as the Monument Pool or the long run after the rapids below the Monument Pool, (called Island Run), the browns hug the bank and often cruise when they feed. I once watched a fisherman repeatedly cast to the same spot in the slow-moving slack water off Island Run. A fish had risen there earlier and the angler obviously hoped that it would rise there again. Nevertheless, I was certain that the fish was cruising, or as some say "striding" the stretch, and was now rising downstream from him. If he hadn't been with a guide, I would have politely suggested that he move downstream, watch the sequence of rises, and cast just ahead of the last rise. Either he was a difficult client who didn't heed the advice of his guide or the guide was a poor one.

Art Lee wrote a two-part article on the Ausable that appeared in the mid- and late-season issues of *Fly Fisherman* in 1975 and spoke disparagingly about the small stocked-rainbows in the shorter no-kill section that existed at that time. He wrote that he stalked the bigger wild browns, which lived upstream in a slow water section, referred to as the Ausable Flats, char-acterized by bends, log jams, and over-hanging brush.

Today, there are big fish throughout the river, but the biggest wild ones are

MIKE ZELIE

*Scott Daniels casting to cruising browns in the Ausable's Island Run.*

in the waters just above the dam at Wilmington and below the dam in Bush Country, a section with limited access and tough wading. A six-pound brown was caught just above the dam in the early Spring of 2000, and, my wife, Melody, lost a hog several weeks later in the first rapids above the dam. Mike Zelie caught a 25-inch rainbow on a big stonefly nymph in Bush Country in 1999, casting upstream from the bank into pocket-water.

While the chances of catching big fish are greatest below Wilmington, the river is fast with poor footing between boulders. A wading staff, while required for safety, is not much help because a safe place to put both feet is difficult to find, and, when found, you can end up facing in the wrong direction. Bank fishing is the best alternative in many stretches.

Like most freestone streams, the smaller, younger fish live in the upper sections of the river, with the water above the ski jumps being the nursery section. For the beginning angler, the area below Route 73 at the Iron Bridge is heavily stocked and many fish can be seen rising during a hatch. Standing on the bridge, I watched an elderly couple cast and cast to rising fish with only occasional success. When the man remarked to me that he couldn't figure out what they were taking, I suggested that he switch from his floating caddis pattern to a Green Emerger. His wife heard me and waded over to bushes along the bank to examine their branches. "Sure enough," she said. "The fly was a green one." They both switched to an emerging pattern and were instantly into fish.

When leaves turn in the fall, the Adirondack region is breathtaking. After a long hot summer, a trip to the West Branch in autumn is rejuvenating,

*Scott Daniels with a typical brown from the Ausable's South Flats.*

but it can get very cold. One fall, the temperature fell below freezing during the third week in September when we were staying in the state campground on the river. Luckily for me, my tent partner, Bob Young, brought a propane heater. Although Tom and Scott warned us that our tent might burn up, we both stayed toasty-warm while they shivered throughout the long night. The fish must have been cold, too, because we caught nothing in the morning and left to watch anglers fishing for landlocked salmon below the dam on the Bouquet River in Willsboro.

## Some Interesting Characters

The price we paid for swapping stories with other anglers at the Adirondacks Sports Shop was usually the purchase of Fran Betters' flies—the Ausable Wulff, Haystack, Usual, and Mini-muddler patterns, all flies he originated. In his later years, Fran rarely participated in our conversations, usually remarking, "I haven't been out much lately, but customers say it's been really good—March Browns all over the water!" For Fran it was always *really good* and March Browns were the flies he was currently tying. In fact, I always suspected that Fran believed that if he tied up enough flies of a specific imitation that the natural would begin rising on the river!

Fran was born on the river and his father, who fished with Ray Bergman, taught him to fly-fish. I am sure Fran did catch 20-inch fish in the river as he was a skilled pocket-water fisherman, probably catching some of them in the pool behind his fly shop named Better's Pool. In his younger days, Fran would tell us, without glancing up from his tying bench, he'd caught a 20-inch fish the evening before we arrived, resulting in our predictable disappointment when none of us caught a trout anywhere near that size. Of course, had we been smarter, we would have realized that Fran was in his shop most evenings well after dark and had little time to fish. Either he was tying flies or working on one of the newspaper columns he wrote to supplement his income. In 1978, Fran, together with William Philips, authored the *Fisherman's Map of the West Branch of the Ausable*. Fran also published *Fishing the Adirondacks* in 1982. His article on the West branch appeared in Dennis Aprill's edited book, *Good Fishing in the Adirondacks*. Fran also self-published a small volume of mystery stories that can be purchased in his fly shop.

Fran was usually tying flies when I entered his shop and his typical response to "I need a net" was, without looking up, "I know there is one around here because I saw some last week. Give me a moment to think and I'll come up with one." He always sounded annoyed when you wanted something he couldn't immediately put his hands on, which was almost everything, except the flies he was currently tying. To say that his shop was extremely disorganized was an understatement! I believe he liked to keep it that way to give it character, deliberately patterning it after one operated for more than 50 years by the colorful Jimmie Deven, owner of the Angler's Roost in New York City. (Deven kept Abercrombie & Fitch stocked with fly-fishing supplies from his exceptionally cluttered store until the famous department store stopped selling them.)

Some anglers, unfamiliar with Better's style of relating, used to remark that Fran thought he was *better* than others and perhaps that was how his family got their name. Actually betters were hitching posts around which were wound the inborn cables on a clipper ship, a fitting name for a spot where many of us stopped off to meet old friends.

Fran's daughter took over his shop in the mid-1990s and it was so neat that I didn't recognize it! Nets were even sorted by size, material, and design. It wasn't the same place! On my last visit, I was told that his daughter was gone, he had leased the place for a year to another operator, and now he was back! I was assured of the truth of this claim by a big sign in front of the store saying, "Fran is Back."

There are now two other fly shops in Wilmington. One is at the Hungry Trout Motor Inn and Restaurant. Anglers staying in the motel can fish its private waters downstream from Wilmington. The other shop, located at the Wilmington Bridge on Route 86, opened in March of 2000. I stopped in the shop for the first time in the Spring of 2000, looking for a deli sandwich. To my surprise the first floor of the building no longer housed the White Face Market, where I bought deli sandwiches for nearly 30 years, but instead a new fly shop called the Ausable River Sport Shop. I was bemoaning the fact that there were three fly shops in the area and not a single deli when I discovered that the proprietor, who was sitting at a tying vise, was Kevin Henebry, a fishing partner of mine in the late 1970s and early 1980s. Kevin informed me that he had operated Fran's shop for a year but had moved to his own location when Fran decided to come out of retirement.

Kevin and I had lost touch after we both moved to different locations in the state. In addition to regular visits to Catskill streams, Kevin and I fished together for bonefish in March of 1979 in the waters off Little Exuma in the Bahamas. Our 67-year-old guide, Gloria Patience, was known throughout the islands as "Tiger Lady" because of her skills at catching tiger sharks. In addition, she was honored in the Bahamas in 1977 as "Glamorous Granny of the Year," having nine children and 17 grandchildren. She was one of 11 bonefish guides in the Exumas at the time, the oldest of whom was 80, but she was the only one who was white. Gloria guided Jack Nicklaus to victory in the 1976 Fly-Casting Division of the Bahama Bonefish Bonanza Tournament hosted by the Club Peace and Plenty, one of the island's four small hotels.

Before she became a commercial fisherman and fishing guide, Gloria ran a massage parlor called the Pilot House Club. As Gloria Lawless, after her first husband who later passed away, she was well-known to many celebrities. Whenever a movie was shot in Nassau, Gloria massaged its stars. Kirk Douglas, Elizabeth Taylor, Ida Lupino, Ava Gardner, and Howard Duff were among her regular customers. When Howard Hughes was living at the Emerald Beach Hotel in 1954, he had a regular appointment with Gloria and she was one of the few people he talked to. Gloria and her second husband dined with Mr. and Mrs. Nixon on the eve of Nixon's loss to John Kennedy in 1960.

Fleix Wells, 75 at the time and a long-time friend of Gloria's, used to catch bonefish up to 42 inches on hand lines. One 42-inch bone he beached took out 18 fathoms of handline, never allowing Wells to loop the line around the pole he drove into the bank for this purpose. It forced him to follow it up the shoreline and he stumbled along the mangroves as he went. Wells was around when hand lines were made out of Sisal, a plant in the same family as that used to make Manila Rope. In his youth, schools of bones between 36- and 46-inches were seen regularly in the Exumas. They disappeared after dynamite became a popular method to capture fish and after commercial seekers of crayfish started using bleach to seize their prey. They dumped large quantities of bleach into the water, causing the crayfish to float to the surface, but also causing the death of everything else in the area and forcing the larger fish to flee.

Kevin and I didn't use Gloria much, however, because a storm made the flats inhospitable during our five-day trip. We stayed at Red Hill Plantation where we were guests of the owners, Ray and Bea Fitzgerald, parents of Kevin's wife Sherry. Ray kept us entertained with stories of his Scottish ancestors, five of whom were hung from the Tower of London following the Irish Rebellion. His grandfather was one of four brothers sent by the British to colonize the islands. As a boy, Ray was the only white child among the 139 black children with whom he attended school.

I first met Kevin in the early 1970s in the Sunset Sporting Goods store in New Paltz, New York. He was selling his hand-tied flies to Tony Tantillo, the store's colorful owner. Tony put his store up for sale once, and when I responded, he told me I didn't really want to own a store. He said people break into the store regularly to steal guns, he had been held up once with one of his own guns, he spent excessive time filling out government forms and small business surveys, he worked from sunup until sundown, and at the year's end, he pocketed only $7,000! With a sales pitch like that, it's no wonder he still owns the store.

Tony was one of the first anglers to regularly catch big browns at night along the shoreline of the Pepacton Reservoir instead of rowing out, as did so many others under lantern light, into 30 or 40 feet of water to lower big baitfish to the bottom. He likes to tell of the time when he and his girlfriend were making-out in his tent at the reservoir's edge when his shoreline rig made the telltale noise which signaled that a big fish had engulfed the ten-inch baitfish. He said that for a brief moment he was torn between staying with his girlfriend or grabbing the rod and fighting the fish. He reported that the choice was simple — his girlfriend would still be there after the fish was caught, but the fish wouldn't be there if he waited to finish their amorous activities. I often wondered if this was a fishing story or one about his masculine prowess.

I told Tony that if I had chosen a fish over my girlfriend, I would have found the tent empty when I returned. And I could also lose the fish. Tony smiled and replied, "I make sure I keep the car keys, and I am very apologetic, as well as very patient!"

I subsequently learned that Kevin was raised in Carmel, New York, where he sold worms at the age of five to anglers visiting Lake Carmel. When he was older he fished both the East and West Branches of the Croton River, catching large browns during their fall spawning runs. Kevin first fished the Ausable in the 1960s when he was a student at Paul Smith's College in nearby Saranac Lake, and he has returned every year since to fish its turbulent waters.

### Melody's Big Fish

On Saturdays throughout the season, starting at noon, Kevin holds two-hour casting sessions at his house just up the street from his store and Sherry serves a barbecue lunch prior to the instructional sessions. I left Melody at Kevin's home for the session and fished the river downstream from the Wilmington Dam. The weather had turned cold and no fish were working for the few flies that hatched during this period.

RICH GARFIELD

*Melody with an Ausable rainbow.*

When the instructional session was over, I signed up Melody to fish Sunday afternoon with Rich Garfield, a guide who works out of Kevin's shop. Rich asked if I could give Melody one of my reels, noting during the casting session that her line was full of kinks. Unfortunately, the reel that I planned to lend her had cracked and worn line. Since it was a double taper I reversed it, but I did not have the patience to tie a nail knot between the line and the backing. Rich had told me that he rarely took anglers to the Ausable, but instead took them to other nearby streams where it was less crowded but often just as productive. Because it was overcast and cold, he said he couldn't guarantee that Melody would catch any fish, but he would guarantee that she would learn to read the water, select the appropriate fly, learn to tie it on correctly, and cast to holding spots. Consequently, I assumed that a secure nail knot was unnecessary and tied another knot.

Rich fooled me and took Melody to a secluded spot on the Ausable above the two-mile-long lake formed by the Wilmington Dam. After several casts, she was into a big fish—a wild brown

well over 20 inches that immediately made a long run downstream and striped off all her line. My hastily-tied knot failed and the line disconnected from the backing and floated downstream. She cried out to Rich, "What do I do now?" He stepped into the stream, grabbed the line, and ran downstream after the running fish, with Melody close behind. When the fish tired, he and Melody hand-stripped in the line, but it became tangled around Rich's feet and the big fish broke off after a jump and another run.

Exasperated by this frustrating experience, they sat down on the riverbank and cursed me out. Both were extremely annoyed. Melody, because a competitive spirit had suddenly emerged from her hidden depths and Rich, because, after all, not many eastern guides put a novice angler into a wild fish over 20 inches! After they both cooled down Melody caught several nice fish, but these experiences were anticlimactic. The story of her big fish appeared in the *Lake Placid News* on June 15, 2000. It began on the first page with a picture of her with a rainbow she caught and continued in the *Wilmington Life* section, but the author, Lee Manchester, taking writers' liberty, reported that she actually caught the fish and implied that it was pictured on the front page of the paper.

### The Ausable in the Old Days

Anglers often dream about fishing rivers before they were crowded with anglers and depleted of big native fish. Ausable anglers are no exception. But unlike Catskill streams, where anglers came in the 1830s to stay in boarding homes or even large hotels to fish for native brook trout, the Ausable and its tributaries were not heavily fished until the early 1900s.

*Where did that big fish go?*

Historically, the Adirondacks was a place where not only the poor got poorer, but where many of the rich got poorer. The tenants of land barons fought the unrelenting resistance of the land to their farming efforts. The lean soil, hard winters, and miserly growing season took their toil. In addition, few roads existed for the enduring survivors to help take their world from subsistence into a market economy. Because their tenants could not pay their rents, many landowners became land-poor. Alexander Macomb, who owned almost four million acres in 1791, died in debtors' prison, driven somewhat mad by the disparity between his landholding and his cash in hand. By 1840 so many struggling farmers had left the mountain valleys that only four families remained in the Ausable River town of North Elba.

But other rich got richer in a land so rugged that it was among the last in the lower 48 states to be surveyed, a land that had been the eastern corridor for bloody frontier wars. Indians fought Indians, French fought British, and the Colonists and their allied Indian tribes fought the English and their allied Indian tribes. Legend has it that the word Adirondack means "to eat bark," an insult the Iroquois hurled at the Algonquins to deride their woodworking skills. Those who got richer in this inhospitable land were the lumber and iron magnates, whose investments resulted in mining towns, logging camps, and tannery hamlets springing up throughout the mountainous land.

A few anglers did come to the Adirondacks in the 1830s, but they came to fish the lakes, not the streams and rivers. The lakes, unlike the rivers, were noted for big brook and lake trout and most of the rivers had been declared public ways so that lumber could be transported down their currents to lumber mills. After the lumber-starved British Royal Navy discovered the tall, straight white pines in the Adirondack forests—with which to mast its fleet of ships—lumber floated down its rivers in droves. In fact, a skilled river driver could go from one side of a river to the other by hoping from log to log and never see the water. The feeder creeks, home of the native brook trout, were blasted to make channels, and dams were constructed on them when their normal flows were insufficient to move logs. Most of the logging took place within a mile of a stream or river.

But when 15-pound lake trout and five-pound brook trout can be easily caught in a lake, why bother fishing streams for pan-size fish, especially when black flies and mosquitoes eat you alive. On lakes, stiff breezes kept these bugs under control. But equally important, was the nature of these early anglers. They were prominent business men who weren't inclined to hike through rugged woodlands to fish in creeks. Unlike Catskill fishermen, who usually combined a family outing with fishing, these wealthy anglers came with male companions. Initially, the men stayed in boarding homes, but, after marveling at the fish they caught, they bought property on lakes and started private clubs. Women weren't allowed in these clubs because they were viewed as extensions of the exclusive men clubs in New York City.

The first club was the Lake Piseco Trout Club, established in 1840 on 100 acres in Hamilton County by six men who had fished the lake annually for ten years. The lodge at the club, with a room for each member, was called "Walton Hall," after their patron saint Izaak Walton. One club member was Reverend G. W. Bethune, American editor of Izaak Walton's *Compleat Angler*, and he included a report of the club in the 1880 edition. Members of the club weren't men who gave up their stylish lives to rough it for a week. No sir. Hired help transported them to the club, purchased and cooked their food, made their beds, cleaned their building, maintained their grounds, baited their hooks, and netted, cleaned, and iced their fish. All they had to do was reel in the fish, drink, and play cards.

After breakfast each day, the members, each of whom had his own boat and oarsman, would troll the lake using two rods rigged with nine-foot gut leaders. They caught brook trout in the lake itself, using live bait, and lake trout at the lake's outlet, where they often used big wet flies. Fishing at the outlet was infrequent however, because mosquitoes, midges, and black flies in this sheltered area usually kept them away from it. During nine days of June in 1843, the six members took 629 pounds of trout, with individual trout weighing from eight to 12 pounds. The largest was 20 pounds. In 1844, one member caught 44 pounds of trout in one day. Over a five-year period, their recorded catch was two tons of trout.

As a result of heavy fishing, fishing around the parameter of the future Adirondack Park deteriorated as early as 1853. Anglers, used to catching landlocked salmon up to 20 pounds in Lake George and nearby Schroon Lake, reported catching fish that averaged only one pound and a half. Those who once could row across a lake and hook fish easily, now resorted to other methods. These methods included setting up buoys, chumming all around them, and returning shortly thereafter to catch the fish that the chum attracted and spearing the fish at night by torch light when they came into the shores in the fall to spawn.

But sportsmen continued to come to the mountains. Eventually, some of the dirt tracks used by travelers were paved with logs, making access possible to lakes by stage coach, but the ride was a bone-jarring experience. The buckboard, with a long spring board between the front and rear wheels, was invented to make the best of the terrible roads. Railroads were built to cart hemlock bark, iron ore, and pulpwood or massive logs, but the first railroad to bring tourists to the center of the future park wasn't built until 1877 when tracks for the Chateauqay Railroad

*New York's West Canada Creek, first fished by members of the Lake Piseco Trout Club.*

were laid from Plattsburg to Saranac Lake. A ten-mile spur was added to Lake Placid to take convicts to the Dannemore State Prison, and later, to serve the mines in the Lyon Mountains. Eventually passenger cars were added and visitors could travel to Lake Placid. In 1894, the Whitehall and Plattsburg Railroad Company created a spur to the Ausable Forks, enabling anglers, if they really wanted to do so, to fish in the polluted Ausable River. Travelers had few places to stay, but the back country tavern, with its unfinished attic, soon gave birth to the north country inn, and the inn, in turn, gave birth to the double-balconied hotel.

One early inn was the Sportsman's Inn, started by Appollos Smith, first called Pol and later Paul. Smith was a towering Vermonter who worked briefly as an Erie Canal boatman. As a young adult he was attracted to the area by his love for Loon Lake, where he worked as a guide for several years. Guides were essential because guests

were unfamiliar with the territory and had neither the means to get to the best fishing spots nor boats to use when they got there. Guides in those days earned their wages. Smith selected the camping grounds, transported the anglers to it, felled trees, peeled their bark for shanties, constructed balsam beds, erected shelves and racks, gathered wood, built campfires and smudges and kept them going night and day, prepared and cooked meals, washed and dried dishes, and disappeared at night or early in the morning to return with fresh venison or fish.

In 1848 Smith opened a boarding house in Franklin County, hired both his parents to work for him, and offered guests his services as a fishing and hunting guide. He saved the money he earned and, in 1851, bought 2,000 acres on the Saranac River where he built a sporting lodge for up to ten men. He called it "Hunter's Home," but he boarded fishermen as well. The first floor contained a living

*New York's Boquet River below Hillsboro Falls.*

room, kitchen, and a barrel of whiskey with a dipper attached. The cost for room and board in the lodge was $1.25 per day and the cost of the whiskey was 4¢ a drink on the honor system. The second floor was the bunk room.

Landlocked salmon ran up the river from Lake Champlain and Smith had a place where anglers could stay and fish as well as hunt. But the big salmon only inhabited the river in the fall and eventually the river became too full of logs to fish for them. In addition, Smith's guests wanted a place to bring their families, so, in 1858, Smith bought 50 acres on Lower St. Regis Lake and built the Grand Hotel, a 17-room hotel chartered under the Paul Smith Hotel Company, which he later expanded to a 500 room hotel on 30,000 acres, which included ten lakes.

Smith died in 1912 and his son ran the hotel until 1937. He, in turn, willed it to establish a coeducational sectarian college in his father's name, Paul Smith College, with majors in liberal arts, forestry, and hotel management. Kevin

attended the college as a young man and when he wasn't studying, he fished the Ausable River.

More than 200 forges operated in the nineteenth century in the Adirondacks, with many of them located along the iron-russet banks of the Ausable. New York State led the nation in ore production in 1850, with ore from the blast furnaces at Ausable Forks used to form the sides of the Monitor, the famed Civil War ship, and the wires used to suspend the Brooklyn Bridge. The forges needed charcoal to operate and the clear cutting of nearby forests by iron miners was worse than that of the lumbermen.

Charcoal was made in "kilns," a log enclosure in which the wood was deprived of oxygen and slowly burned. Two-and-one-quarter cords of wood were needed to make 100 bushels of charcoal and up to 500 bushels of charcoal were needed to generate one ton of ore. The hills near the river were alive with crashing hardwoods.

Without trees to provide cover, the

snow melted rapidly in the spring and without tree roots to absorb the moisture or to hold the soil, the river ran dirty with silt. It could not have sustained many fish, except in its headwaters, to which there was limited access. The loss of trees also produced other undesirable effects. The opening of the forest created conditions that favored some animals over others. For example, moose disappeared when deer moved into the clearings and multiplied their numbers. Deer carry a parasite that is deadly to moose. In addition, the destruction of beaver ponds by logging activity and killing beavers for their

*A trip down the Ausable Canyon can be enjoyed by all family members.*

pelts, resulted in further losses of beaver ponds and drastically reduced the moose's food supply, forcing them down from the mountains and into the lakes where they were easy prey for hunters.

By the 1890s, the Adirondacks were home to more than 60 private associations and sporting clubs that together controlled hundreds of thousands of acres, the largest being the Adirondack League Club, a club that owned more than 200,000 virgin acres. The Adirondack Mountain Reserve, and its associated Ausable Club, owned 40,000 acres, including the headwaters of the Ausable. Later, the League Club founded the Association for Preservation of the Adirondacks, a group that became a leading advocate for the "forever wild" clause in the state constitution The League Club still owns 50,000 acres and leases another 22,000, which includes 56 lakes and ponds.

The shift from rags to wood pulp in paper marketing brought a whole new world of trees to the woodcutter. Pulp grinding machines didn't care if the wood was crooked or thin, its cellulose was all that was needed. The forests would have been decimated if concerned sporting groups had not pressured the state government to make the area a national preserve. In response to this pressure, both the Adirondack Park and the Catskill Forest preserves were created in 1885 and officially defined in 1892. In 1894 the state constitution was amended to include the statement that state forest preserves were to be "forever kept as wild forest lands."

Charlie Reese, a member of the Adirondack Guide Association that formed in 1891, loved to tell fishing tales about Adirondack Park streams in the early 1900s. He told listeners that anglers didn't carry poles when they hiked into the forest. They took a line and a hook and upon arrival cut an alder branch. Charlie reported that some didn't even bother with a rod. They brought a large cut-open syrup can with a rope attached, threw it in the stream, and simply scooped out the brook trout.

### Other Adirondack Waters

In addition to the Ausable, other nearby rivers, creeks, and ponds provide good angling. Anglers visiting in late September can try for landlocked salmon running up either the Bouquet or the Saranac Rivers from Lake Champlain. Tom Royster landed an eight-plus-pound landlocked and lost a much bigger one on the Boquet below the Willsboro Dam in the fall of 2002. Lake George also has a healthy population of landlocks and lake trout, with a small population of rainbows. The 28,000-acre lake, known as the Big G, receives almost no surface water as it is fed by gigantic underground springs and is extremely clear. The Lake George Association, an organization of residents, assists sanitary inspectors to enforce the strict sanitary codes to keep it that way.

I also recommend fishing the bays across from Diamond Point and the mouth of Northwest Bay Brook. Cast large red and white saddle hackle streamers tied on a 1/0 saltwater hook and retrieve them slowly along the bottom. When they stop, or you feel a slight tug, raise the rod tip sharply and be prepared for the first run of the fish Josselyn called the River Wolf. Northern pike fight nicely on a fly rod and their medieval appearance contrasts sharply with the salmon. A large smallmouth, searching the shallows for food prior to spawning, might also be hooked in a bay, although most will be sleeping, stacked up like cord-wood along the drop-offs.

### Accommodations and Other Activities

Along Route 86 south of Wilmington, and in Wilmington itself, visitors have a choice of many motels. I usually stay at the Alpine Inn (518-946-2263) right in Wilmington. Those wanting the company of other fishermen can stay at the Hungry Trout (518-946-2217) and fish their private waters. Two motels at the base of Whiteface Mountain are the North Pool Campground and Motor Inn (800-245-0288) and the Four Seasons Motor Lodge (518-946-2247). The state operates the Wilmington Notch State Campground (518-946-7172), with 54 small sites in the same general location.

My companions and I usually eat at R. F. McDougal's Tavern which is associated with the Hungry Trout. When I am with my wife, I eat at two restaurants located along Route 86, just south of Wilmington—the Wilderness Inn and the Sportsman Inn, the latter being part of a motel by the same name. The restaurant at the Sportsman Inn has as plaque on the wall that holds numerous wet flies tied by old-time river fishermen and another one, taken from the side of a barn, that contains the silhouettes of big trout caught in the river. In Lake Placid, the angler can choose from among many hotels, including a Best Western Inn, Hilton Hotel, Holiday Inn, and Howard Johnsons, some of which feature evening entertainment.

From the Village of Wilmington, anglers can drive up the Whiteface Memorial Highway where they can access the summit of White Face Mountain by trail or elevator for a panoramic view of the Adirondacks. A weather museum crowns the summit. Just before the toll gate to the Memorial Highway, children can fish a small pond for rainbow trout. About halfway up to the toll gate, anglers can turn left on a paved road and find a number of trailheads where both short and long walks can be taken that provide views of the river valley. Santa's Workshop, which claims to be the nation's first theme-park is also off this road, a place where your children can get a personalized magic wand.Visitors can take the Whiteface Mountain chair-lift ride at the entrance to the ski resort off Route 86 as an alternative to driving up the Memorial Highway.

Along the Ausable, both High Falls Gorge and the Ausable Canyon can be visited. I highly recommend taking the cruise through the canyon. It is impressive. The canyon has been open to visitors since the 1870s, when Winslow Homer and other famous artists painted along the river.

The town of Lake Placid, primarily a tourist village, is less than eight miles from the river. The Community Theater Players perform at the Lake Placid Center for the Arts, located just north of the village. There is a movie theater, a number of fine restaurants, and a variety of gift shops. The Winter Olympics have been held twice in Lake Placid and various structures created for these competitions can be visited. From Holiday Harbor, scenic cruises can be taken on Lake Placid. Motor boats can be rented to navigate the lake or paddle boats to enjoy the much smaller Mirror Lake which is stocked with rainbows. Mountain bikers and joggers prowl the village streets and the surrounding roads, and special events are held for them throughout the summer.

Lake Placid hosts the home and grave of John Brown, the famous abolitionist, hung in 1859 after his raid on Harper's Ferry, Virginia. The song "John Brown's Body" was probably the most popular union rallying song during the Civil War. The grandfather of Langston Hughes, who I quote in the first chapter, traveled with John Brown. The Lake Placid Historical Museum occupies the old Penn Central Railroad Station and the W. Alton Jones Cell Science Center, the permanent home of the Tissue Culture Association, is located in the village.

A short drive west of Lake Placid to Saranac Lake is the Trudeau Institute Research Laboratories. Anglers can see the Little Red Cottage, where Dr. Trudeau initiated his work on tuberculosis, as well as a statue of the famous doctor by Gutzon Borglum, the sculptor of Mount Rushmore. Nearby is the Will Rogers Hospital, famous for treating patients with respiratory diseases. The Robert Lewis Stevenson Cottage also is located in Saranac Lake. The novelist spent the winter of 1887-88 recuperating from tuberculosis while he wrote the draft of *The Master of Bailantrees*.

Information on Lake George, the Hudson River and its tributaries, and Thirteenth Lake, an excellent salmon fishery, can be obtained from the Warren County Department of Tourism (Department 872, Municipal Center, Lake George, New York, 12485). Those planning a fall visit Plattsburg can obtain a Saranac River map from the Lake Champlain Chapter of Trout Unlimited (P.O. Box 2615, Plattsburg, NY, 12901). The salmon in this river are big, with many up to eight pounds. Cruises can be taken on Lake Champlain and day trips taken across the lake to Burlington, Vermont.

# CHAPTER THREE

# The Battenkill
## *The Perfect Freestone Stream*

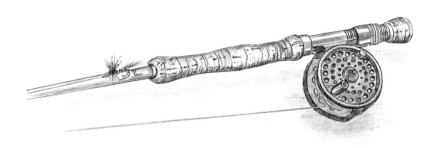

In the 1970s, I bought a share in a lot on the banks of the Battenkill on public waters near Shushan, New York. The lot was owned by 14 anglers who called themselves the Battenkill Fly Fishers and they were looking to fill a vacancy created by a departed member. I was invited by the group to fish by the lot before my purchase was approved. I immediately fell in love with the river and the Green Mountains through which it flowed. I considered it a perfect trout stream—a clear, deep, free-stone stream that received considerable water from underground sources and did not change its level after every rain shower. And best of all, its trout were all wild.

At the time, I knew nothing of the 'Kill's history, but the half dozen brook and brown trout I took on my trial visit was all I needed to know about the river. In the mile of water above and below the lot were long riffles and runs, deep pools, shaded back-water sections, some of which were spring-fed, hemlock-lined banks, and crystal-clear water, even after strong rains. The pebble bottom was easy to wade, yet the current was swift and the fish grew muscular and strong. Unlike the Ausable, or even the Beaverkill, both of which have steeper gradients, there were no clearly defined step pools, rapids, or sections of boulder-strewn pocket-water.

The second weekend in May was set aside for an annual lot cleanup. The work typically involved clearing the lot of debris, trimming trees, repairing the steep driveway, and setting up the picnic tables. We took a brake from these chores to fish the Hendrickson hatch that, like clockwork, came off at 2:00 and lasted until about 3:30. It was the river's best hatch and it brought up fish that we wouldn't see again the whole year. Thanks to Ron Steenrod, originator of the famous Hendrickson dry fly, and Art Flick, whose Red Quill imitated the male fly, I always took several fish about 14 inches during this hatch.

Don Phillips, the originator of boron fly rods and a founding member of the group, was president of the organization when I joined. Don first learned about the properties of boron as an aerospace engineer. Don left the aerospace field and started his own company, Fly Craft, producing rods and blanks using composite material designs for which he obtained U. S. patents. Don has retired but he continues to write articles and books on rods and rod design. His books include *An In-Depth Look at the Design of the Modern Fly Rod: Its History and Its Role in Fly Fishing*, *The Technology of Fly Rods*, and *What Fly Rod is Best for You*.

## Lessons Learned on the 'Kill

Lee Wulff, who once lived on the New York 'Kill very close to our lot and who promoted the river in his early writings, credited the Battenkill with giving him new insights. Like Wulff, I too have learned a lot from this storied New England river. In the mid-1970s, my use of the dry fly, and the fly paste that floated it higher, decreased dramatically. One day, a strong wind during the Hendrickson hatch blew hundreds of flies from the tree limbs into the river. To my surprise, all the flies safely floated downstream over fish who continued to feed on emerging nymphs. Since them, I rarely use a dry fly when fish are rising and my catch rate during a hatch has improved dramatically. I also imparted a little movement to a deer-hair emerger pattern I created for this very purpose.

## Light and Sound

The Battenkill taught me the valuable lesson of bright sunlight on the water. I usually had good luck in the early morning, drifting nymphs downstream into the eddies behind the large boulders that hugged the shoreline. A bright orange brown, between 10 and 12 inches, would flash and inhale my nymph as it floated past a rock, even when no flies were on the water. But as soon as a boulder was no longer in the shade, all action stopped. I moved to the Hemlock-lined sections of the river where fish would usually chase a skittered caddis imitation or to the riffle water where I would cast nymphs upstream.

The Battenkill taught me about the keen senses of fish. One day in late July, when the river was low, I was standing on one of the V-framed cribbings, built by the state of New York in an effort to improve fish-holding lies. I was watching several trout feeding on small flies just above the cribbing. About 100 yards upstream, an angler rounded the bend. Both fish scooted for cover. They say that when an elephant stomps his feet to warn others of his species, that the vibrations can be heard by other elephants up to 30 miles away. From that time forward, I never fished downstream when the water was low.

## Tolerance for Others

The Battenkill taught me to respect all fishermen regardless of the first impression they make on me. One thing I always enjoyed about fishing the Battenkill was inspecting the gear of fellow fishermen. Unlike the Esopus, which I fished regularly, the Battenkill was the fashion plate of trout streams. The Orvis Company was located on the river and most visiting anglers purchased equipment from it. When Orvis first sold the chest pack as an alternative to the fishing vest, I would see it on the 'Kill long before I would see it elsewhere. I never saw it on the Esopus. Esopus Creek anglers would fall down from laughter if they saw an angler with a chest pack. From a distance, they might mistake the angler for a pregnant woman.

The Battenkill is where I first saw anglers seine the river and tie exact imitations of the nymphs they found, reminding me of the story of the transformation of the Woggle-Bug in the *Land of Oz*. For those unfamiliar with the Bug's story, let me retell it to you; first I will quote from the Bug who describes his transformation.

One day a marvelous circumstance occurred that altered my very existence and brought me to my present state of greatness. The Professor discovered me in the act of crawling across the hearth and before I could escape he had caught me between his thumb and forefinger.

"My dear children," said, he, I have captured a Woggle-Bug—a very rare and interesting specimen. Do any of you know what a Woggle-Bug is?"

"No!" yelled the scholars, in chorus.

"Then," said the professor, "I will get out my magnifying glass and throw the insect upon a screen in a highly magnified condition, so that you may all study carefully its peculiar construction and become acquainted with its habits and manner of life."

He then brought from the cupboard a most curious instrument, and before I could realize what happened

I found myself thrown upon a screen in as highly magnified state.

The Bug goes on to describe how some of the scholars, frightened by his magnified image, fainted. During the commotion that followed, the Bug realized that this was his opportunity to escape. He was proud of his now giant size and realized that he now could travel anywhere safely in the world and be a fit associate for those he might chance to meet. The bug remarks:

I have never ceased to congratulate myself for escaping while I was highly magnified, for even my excessive knowledge would have proved of little use to me had I remained a tiny, insignificant insect.

The fisherman who seines the rivers, carries home specimens, studies them under magnifying glasses, and ties exact imitations, should pay heed to the Woggle-Bug's story. Trout will mouth anything that vaguely resembles food. They eat caddisflies in their cases and snails in their shells, strike my leader link, inhale hail in the winter, and eat hamburger and bread tossed in the water. Most caddisflies hatch at night, but I still catch lots of fish on caddis imitations.

## The Elusive Big Fish

The Battenkill taught me that I will probably never catch a really big native trout on a fly. I have snorkeled much of the river, but the only really big fish I have seen were suckers—any big brown residents must have heard me coming and quickly departed. Nonetheless, I know they are there because I have heard their large kirplunks and have seen several come completely out of the water for a dragon fly in midsummer. Without success, I have skated, danced, and sailed dragon fly imitations where I saw these big fish jump. I have even fished at night with both a large wet fly, Joe Humphrey's style, and, in desperation, with a Rapala, but I have never hooked one of the huge ones. Bob once worked a salted minnow without a hook through waters that we knew contained big fish and none hit the bait.

Some angling writers attribute the switch in trout habits from day-to-nighttime feeding to increased human activity on the river during the day. I don't believe this explanation. Big browns are meat-eating predators and predators gain an advantage over their prey when they eat at night. White-tip sharks, for example, lie lazily on the reef's bottom during the day while countless fish swim around them. At night, they become active and forage for these same fish, seeking them while they lie peacefully in their sleeping places within the coral.

John Randolph, editor of *Fly Fisherman*, lived on the Battenkill for 15 years during which time the magazine was published in Manchester. In his correspondence with me, he wrote:

According to fisheries biologists, who had baseline data going back to the '40s, the Battenkill is one of the top producing wild brown trout rivers in eastern North America. Its pools and runs during the period (1970-1982) were full of healthy, wild browns, with brook trout occupying about a 10% niche. Yet, the brook trout were caught at a rate twice that of the browns. It works out that wild browns, especially big ones, are too smart for fly-fishers to catch, or even bait and spin fisherman, for that matter.

At the time, fly-fishers complained bitterly (stocking of the New York 'Kill had just been halted) that there were no fish left in the river. I followed the Vermont biologists (with Dick Finlay of Orvis) as they netted the river in August (after most of the sportfish harvest) and I was astounded. The bottom of the 'Kill was literally carpeted with wild, fat browns—of all sizes. You could not find a more healthy population of trout, yet fishermen were absolutely convinced that the fish were not in the river because they did not freely rise to hatches and because they were not willing to rise at 3:30 p.m. The big, medium-sized, and small fish were there, but in the minds of fishermen, if they cannot be seen or caught, they do not exist.

Native Americans say that "the fisherman who never catches anything never will if he keeps complaining that he is unlucky because this spirit will take him to where no fish are." In this case the fish were there, but their spirit was more powerful than that of the typical fisherman.

But I know one angler who got lucky. I have a picture of two large browns (six and four pounds) cut out from the local newspaper that recorded the success of this local angler. He had been driving by the river when he saw a huge splash under a tree overhanging the bank. The first splash was followed by slightly smaller, but equally impressive one immediately downstream. He watched for a while and was about to leave when the events reoccurred. He discovered two very large browns feeding on tree frogs that were periodically falling from the tree into the water. He quickly drove home, took a small rubber frog from his bass box, and returned to the river. He cast the rubber frog under the tree and got his picture in the paper!

Members of our group used to keep a running log of their fishing success. The biggest fish recorded during a five-year period in the 1980s was an 18-inch brown taken at dusk on a Rapala by the son of a member. Howard Weldon, President of our association for over 25 years, has caught three 18-inch browns and half a dozen 17-inch fish on the river, and I watched lot member Bob Kammer hook and land a 17-inch brown, but we stopped keeping the log when the fishing deteriorated.

## The River and Its Environment

The Battenkill taught me about the pulse of a freestone stream, its cycles, and the fragility of its surrounding environment. We used to catch brook trout up to 12 inches in the 1970s, but following a flood in the mid-1980s, six years passed before we caught brookies again. Three years passed before we began to catch browns more than 12 inches. Reluctantly, some of us drove downstream and fished for stockies below Eagleville Bridge. Floods and drought wreak havoc on trout, something we don't notice when we fish rivers that are heavily stocked each year.

During long weekends, I felt no rush to catch fish, like I did when fishing after work. I had time to breath in the surrounding countryside. The Green Mountains through which the 'Kill flows are amply named. Chestnuts and maples have a blush of green haloed in the early morning sun. On cloudy days a mist hangs like gossamer curtains to blue the shadows. I learned to sit on the riverbank and watch the river flow by me or listen to the splatter of rain drops on the broad leaves of the

hickory trees beneath which I took shelter. I sat on a large rock and watched other anglers at work, not to learn from them, but to take pleasure in their success and to let the river reactivate my dreams. The poet Mary Oliver once wrote:

It is the nature of stone to be satisfied.
It is the nature of water to want to be somewhere else.

Like the rock upon which I sat, I was satisfied to simply take in the surrounding environment. Other anglers assisted me in this rejuvenating process, encouraging me to stop and enjoy the roses. One morning, a fisherman, upstream from me, gave a sharp whistle to attract my attention and then pointed further upstream. There stood a doe and her fawn drinking from the river, bathed in the morning sunlight. I moved too quickly and they darted away, as if they had springs in their feet.

## A River in Trouble

The Battenkill taught me to be skeptical of fly shop owners, even when I knew them for long periods. When I actively fished the Battenkill in the 1970s and 1980s, the Angler's Nook, owned by George Schlotter, was a stone's throw from our lot. I would always stop in George's shop to ask him about the fishing. First, he would ask me how I had done, knowing that I sometimes stopped in after fishing. If I did well, as I did in the early 1980s, then he would tell me that others also had done well. If I had not done well, as was the case in the early 1990s, he would tell me that some anglers had done well the week before.

Our experience suggested that the fishing on the Battenkill had been

*The Battenkill—as beautiful in February as it is in June.*

getting worse each year, but George would not support our impressions, reporting that it was good last week or that it would pick up next week. I recently ran into George at the Housatonic Meadows Fly Shop in Cornwall Bridge, Connecticut. He had closed the Angler's Nook and retired from the retail business, but he still tied flies and sold them wholesale. He was delivering flies to old customers and soliciting new ones. George finally admitted that the fishing had become so poor on the Battenkill that he had to close his store. He prefaced his remarks with "Look, John, I'll finally be honest with you!" How many years had he been fooling me into thinking I

had been on the river at the wrong time? Or how many years had he been fooling himself? Yet, knowing that George will no longer be in his shop, tying up the small green fuzzy caddis imitation I often used to fool wary fish, will make the river less hospitable.

By now we know that the "Kill is in serious trouble. Articles in outdoor magazines have reported Vermont's efforts to restore the 'Kill to its once proud place among New England streams. Hopefully, New York will do the same. Yet corrective action requires knowing causes and the cause of the rivers demise is unknown. Some blame it on the aluminum hatch, the large number of canoes that travel the river

*Bill Tucker working downstream on the Battenkill.*

throughout the spring and whose occupants often push fallen logs off the banks to clear their way, resulting in the destruction of undercut banks. The canoes also scrape the bottom in riffled sections, scattering the fish and perhaps killing nymph life. Others blame it on tubers, who float the water in the summer months from sunup to well after sundown and who drag their tubes through shallow riffles, killing the aquatic life that resides there and restricting the feeding opportunities of trout.

Others say that high water conditions have scored the bottom and washed away the structure that supports fish. Sections of the river have become silted up over the years and as a result, significantly fewer insects are available for the trout to eat. State of Vermont fisheries biologists believe just the opposite. They believe that, because of clean up efforts mandated by the U. S. Clean Water Act, the river no longer receives the nutrients it needs to produce a food chain that results in abundant trout. Contrary to popular belief, sewage run-off is not necessarily harmful to fish, and in some cases it is beneficial. Upgrading of septic tanks along a river's bank, while it may make a river cleaner, may remove the nutrients necessary to produce large amounts of aquatic life.

I believe that the state of New York contributed to the river's recent problems when they built the log cribbings

I mention earlier. When the cribbings were first built, I caught good-sized fish both behind and in front of them. Now they are silted up and fish hold no where near any of them. Cribbings, in contrast to natural structures, create environments where fish are easier to catch and, therefore, contribute to over harvesting and depletion of fish. It is much easier for both a spin and a fly-fisherman to cast to the calm water behind a V-crib than to place a lure or float a fly through the branches of a fallen tree. If I had a dollar for every trout I have heard rising unseen under fallen logs, I'd be a rich man today. Even though only one trophy-size fish is allowed in New York's special regulation section, a good spin-fishermen, taking one large fish per day, can remove the larger brood stock from this fragile river in several seasons.

I vividly recall one May weekend when the water was high and it was too deep to wade effectively. Below our lot was a narrow section of the river where a log and rock cribbing lined the bank on our side for about 20 yards. Spring floods and a fallen tree eventually destroyed the upper section of this cribbing. High waters then washed away a large portion of the bank behind the cribbing, creating a new channel, with the cribbed section turning into an island. When the river was high in May, several inches to a foot of water would flow over the upper end of the island cribbing. After it flowed around and over the cribbing, the water in the new channel moved appreciably slower than water in the main channel. As a result, during the Hendrickson hatch, trout would move into the new channel and lay behind the island. As flies were swept over the island, the trout would simply rise up from the slower water behind it and

easily capture them, an effortless way to feed.

Easing myself down the new bank and into the new channel, I could cast into the shallow water that flowed over the island and capture the trout feeding there as easily as they captured flies. I brought to the net four 14-inch browns and a number of smaller fish the first May this opportunity presented itself, easily out-fishing my fellow lot owners who were struggling with the high water in other river sections.

State of Vermont electrofishing studies, more recent than those mentioned by John Randolph, reveal the decline in wild fish. On three sections of the river between 1994 and 1998, populations of wild browns over six inches ranged from nearly 200 per mile to 400 per mile, down from about 700 per mile between 1988 and 1993. But even the 700 per mile at the end of the 1980s was low in comparison to other rivers. Montana's Bighorn River has 6,000 per mile! In addition, a Vermont newspaper reported that fish catches in the Battenkill dropped from well over 12,000 fish in 1988 to 2,000 in 1999 and that the number of fish above ten inches was down by almost 90%. In April of 2000, regulations were changed to catch-and-release along the entire Vermont stretch while awaiting answers from biologists who continue to study the river.

Things may be looking up, however, because Francis Becker reported at our annual meeting in 2001 that he landed several fish exceeding 16 inches the previous year on dry flies, even though his total catch was small. In the spring of 2003, two dead 20-inch browns floated into the eddy by our lot. Inspection revealed that one had been killed by a water bird. Perhaps the other was released by an upstream angler who made no effort to help it survive.

## The 'Kill is Still Worth a Visit

In spite of the river's lost wild trout, I recommend a midweek visit to its beautiful waters and to the magnificent mountain environment through which the 'Kill flows. I can't imagine an angler who wouldn't enjoy the river for its beauty and for the remaining wild fish that it contains. If a visitor wants to catch stocked trout, the stretch below the bridge at Eagleville, New York, is well stocked and in the spring of 2002 spin fishermen caught several holdover browns greater than 20 inches. Above Eagleville, visitors are unlikely to catch large fish or even large numbers of them, but they will catch fish under incredibly rejuvenating conditions. Standing in a shallow riffle, with clear water churning around the feet, and casting above the riffle into the tail of a pool to a rising wild brown, all while casting furtive glances at the sun-drenched Green Mountains, is an experience difficult to duplicate. The closest I have come to doing so was Idaho's Wood River, but that is the subject of another book.

## Accommodations and Other Activities

Anglers who prefer full-service lodges can stay at the Battenkill Lodge (516-671-7690) in Shushan, New York. It has private access to the Battenkill and a stocked pond on the premises where youngsters can catch rainbows. Anglers can camp in Cambridge at the Battenkill Sports Quarters (800-676-8768), located three and a half miles northeast on Route 313 off Highway 22. The closest motels are north of Arlington, Vermont, on Route 7A. Those just south of Manchester include

the Manchester View (800-548-4141), Palmer House Resort (800-917-6245) and Barnstead Inn (800-331-1619).

Several nineteenth-century hotels in Manchester have recently been refurbished, including the white-columned, tower-topped Equinox (800-362-4747) and the Charles Orvis Inn next door to it. The bed-and-breakfast inns in Manchester are too numerous to list here, but one, the Inn at Ormsby Hill (800-670-2841), was the home for 100 years of Edward Isham, Robert T. Lincoln's law partner, and his descendants. A marvelous pancake house in Manchester Village serves delicious buckwheat pancakes, but there are only half-a-dozen tables so be prepared on weekends for a long wait to get served.

Inns in Arlington, the closest to the best fishing spots on the 'Kill, include several with river front property. Those off historic Route 7A are the Hill Farm Inn (800-882-2545), built in 1850 on 50 acres just north of the village; the Keelan House, an 1825 Colonial with one-third of a mile on the river; and the Ira Allen House, an old roadside home with river front property across the road. Others include the Arlington Main House (800-375-6784) on Buck Hill Road, a 1900 Dutch Colonial, and the Arlington Inn (800-443-9442), in central Arlington on route 7A. The inn, the former Green Revival Mansion, was built in 1848 and has been an inn, on and off, since 1889. It includes a restaurant. The other restaurant in Arlington is at the West Mountain Inn on River Road. For a quick bite, visitors can eat at the East Arlington Café.

There are several public campsites in Vermont, but only one is on the river. Camping on the Battenkill (802-375-6663) is in Arlington. The campground at Lake Shaftsbury State Park

(802-375-9978) is located two miles south of Arlington, off Route 7A, and Howell's Camping Area is farther southwest, located at the end of School Street off Highway 313 going east. The National Forest Campground is in the Green Mountain National Forest (802-362-2307) near Manchester, the campground at Emerald Lake State Park (802-362-1655) is in North Dorset, and Hapgood Pond Campground (802-829-6456) is in Peru off Route 11. The Dorset RV Park (802-807-5754) is four miles north of Dorset on Highway 80 and it opens earlier and closes later than the campgrounds (April 15 to October 30).

The Battenkill flows, for part of its length, along the "Antique Corridor" of Vermont's Route 7, the same route that the Housatonic flows along further south in the State of Connecticut. Bennington, Arlington, and Manchester, Vermont, New England towns with rich histories, offer a variety of summer activities that attract families from afar. Bennington, just north of the Massachusetts state line, is the home of Bennington Museum, featuring works of Grandma Moses. Bennington also is home of the Bennington Potters, America's oldest and largest art pottery and Vermont's largest factory outlet for pottery and decorative accessories for the home, and the Bennington Battle Monument, a revolutionary war monument.

Illustrator and painter Norman Rockwell once lived and painted in Arlington and a building has been set aside in this small hamlet to exhibit some of his works. Rockwell died in 1978 in Stockbridge, Massachusetts, not far from the Housatonic River. Between Arlington and Manchester, on Route 7A, Basketville houses a huge collection of hand-crafted baskets and wicker furniture

Hildene, the elegant home of Abraham Lincoln's descendants, is in Manchester Village and it has been open to the public since 1975. There are golf courses and several playhouses in nearby towns such as the Dorset and Weston Playhouses. Melody and I enjoy the used bookstores and art studios in Manchester and I try and hit the Orvis Tent Sale in August.

The Southern Vermont Art Center and The Museum of American Fly Fishing are both in Manchester. The Art Center is a gracious old mansion on 35 acres and it displays paintings, sculpture, prints, and photography. The Museum displays flies tied by Mary Orvis Marbury, author of *Favorite Flies and Their Histories*, and over 1,000 rods and reels made by famous rod makers and owned by the likes of Daniel Webster, Bing Crosby, Ernest Hemingway, and past presidents Hoover and Eisenhower. Northwest of Manchester, on Route 11, is the Bromley Adventure Zone, a winter ski center that offers a variety of summer activities, including cart rides down the mountain slopes.

A vista of the area can be enjoyed by taking a scenic drive up Mt. Equinox or by hiking the six-mile Burr and Burton Trail from Manchester Village. At the top, visitors can stay at the Equinox Mountain Lodge (800-868-6843). Hikers can enjoy the Lye Brook Wilderness, a 14,000-plus-acre preserve south of Manchester. A two-and-a-third-mile trail can be taken to Lye Brook Waterfalls. At the falls, serious hikers can take portions of the Long Trail, a Massachusetts to Quebec path that doubles as the Appalachian Trail.

# CHAPTER FOUR

# The Beaverkill, Willowemoc, and Neversink
## *Fabled Trout Streams*

M any New York City anglers who fished the Beaverkill and Willowemoc during the 1970s and early 1980s used to stop at the H. L. Leonard Shop in Central Valley, just off the thruway exit to Route 17 at Harriman, to ogle and perhaps even to buy a bamboo rod, to bask in the aura of the early Leonard rod makers who moved to New York from coastal Maine—Hiram Leonard, Fred Thomas, Edward Payne, Fred Devine, and Hiram Hawes—or just to get the inside scoop on the Catskill rivers from Ron Kusse, the shop's last manager before it folded.

There was no full-service fly shop near the Beaverkill at the time, but equipment could be purchased at the Little Store in Roscoe and quality flies could be bought at the homes of the Dettes or the Darbees, local husband and wife tiers now enshrined in the Catskill Fly-Fishing Center and Museum located on the banks of the lower Willowemoc between Livingston Manner and Roscoe. Walt Dette invented the Coffin Fly and Harry Darbee the Rat Faced McDougal. Darbee also tied the first fly made entirely of deer hair, later called the Irresistible by Joe Messinger of Morgantown, West Virginia, who tied the identical fly. Ken Lockwood, who used clipped deer hair on a Wulff pattern instead of angora wool, is also said to have invented the fly. Great minds come up with similar ideas!

Henry Darbee descends from one of the areas first residents, Samuel Darbee, who, along with Levi Kindall, settled in 1796 on contiguous farms at the Junction Pool, a now famous angling spot where the Beaverkill and Willowemoc join. Flies can still be bought at both the Darbee House Fly

Shop on old Route 17, and at Dette Trout Flies on Cottage Street in Roscoe, but they are now tied by their offspring.

During this era, I fished the Beaverkill in spots unknown to most anglers and in June in the lower no-kill section between Cooks Falls and Horton. Electrofishing studies had revealed almost no fish outside of no-kill areas by June. I went to the lower section not only because it was less crowded than its upstream counterpart, but also because the Silver Fox Bar and Grill sat right next to it on the river. In between catching and returning stocked trout, I sat at the bar that overlooked the river enjoying a cold beer. I was once joined by a state conservation officer. Sitting beside me, he remarked,

"Well, I'll be damn, would you believe that?"

"Believe what," I said.

"Believe that guy fishing in the river with worms right in front of us."

He left to arrest the guy. When he returned to the bar and to his beer, he shook his head and said, "In all my days, I've never seen such stupidity. There are 'artificial lures only' and 'no-kill' signs posted everywhere and this guy not only uses a worm but he keeps the fish. And he does it right in front of the bar stool upon which I sit. No one has ever made it that easy for me!"

In spite of the numerous articles on fly-fishing for browns on the Beaverkill in the fall, I never had much luck catching the monsters they claim run upstream to spawn. Leaves cover the water and make difficult the floating of a fly. And that's not all. First, spawning trout typically move upstream at night. So my fly usually floated over nothing anyway. Second, browns don't feed during their spawning run. They have

to get annoyed to strike a fly, and they can't get annoyed when I am home sleeping in bed! In late November I have caught some very long, spent trout, but they were so skinny that they resembled pickerel!

One late October, during exceptionally high water, the fish were forced to congregate along the riverbanks. Under these conditions, I stood on the banks and unsuccessfully slung a weighted muddler with added weights upstream behind the large bank boulders along Horse Brook Run. I then switched to a light spin rod and a Rapala and landed four 17-inch browns. The current was so strong, however, that the fish dogged me near the shoreline throughout their brief fight.

## The Upper Willowemoc

During the 1970s and 1980s, while New York City anglers were driving up the thruway and then up Route 17 to fish the Willowemoc Creek, I was driving north from Route 55 on Claryville Road, crossing over the Neversink River on Halls Mills Covered Bridge, a favorite spot of Roy Steenrod, and coming over the mountain on Hunter Road. In the fog, these mountain roads were particularly spooky, but I neither ran into the Headless Horseman nor saw Rip Van Winkle asleep by the roadside. I would cross over the upper Willowemoc on the green steel truss bridge and stop at the fishermen's pull off above the hamlet of De Bruce. I would then walk down the steep bank into the creek. If it had rained and the water was high, I might drive farther upstream and fish just below the confluence of Fir and Butternut Brooks.

I guess I patterned my initial trips to the river after those who first fished the headwaters of the Beaverkill in the

1800s, most of which is now owned by fishing clubs. In 1872 Roscoe, formerly called Westfield Flats, became the terminus of summer passenger service on the Ontario and Western Railroad and the company published a pamphlet in 1878, entitled Summer Homes, that listed boarding homes in the area. Nevertheless, visitors to the region did not typically fish the sections of the rivers that are heavily fished today. The angling season was limited to the hot summer months and fishermen were simply not accustomed to fishing, or even properly equipped to fish, large rivers, a topic I will discuss more fully in later chapters.

Anglers fished the Beaverkill way upstream in Hardenburgh, as opposed to the lower stretches near Roscoe, because brook trout, the preferred trout at the time, were more numerous in the higher elevations where fewer mills cluttered the streams. An early Hardenburgh angler wrote "The Beaverkill is famous for its trout. The water is the clearest and purest, and the trout are abundant and of the finest quality." Mill Brook, Dry Brook, and Furlough Lake, at the head of Dry Brook, were also celebrated fisheries. Owners of boarding houses advertised that the Turnwood, Delhi, and Margaretville Railroads ran within four miles of the town. Inn owners also stressed the good fishing in both Balsam and Tunis Lakes. Tunis Lake got its name from an Indian who was regularly seen carrying led ore out from the woods that he had acquired near the lake at the head of the Beaverkill. Diligent searches failed to locate the mine from which he dug the ore.

As was the case with many Catskill mountain streams, considerably more water ran in the Willowemoc creek in the old days. A lad, fishing with lady friends on the creek at the Shin Creek Falls in the late 1800s, fell into the river and his body wasn't found for two days. I can't imagine losing a body for two days in the upper Willowemoc today.

Fishing writer Ross Kushner calls the upper Willowemoc "Picture Post Card Water" and he is certainly correct. I could fish all but the four-mile stretch owned by the De Bruce Fly Fishing Club. From the last upstream parking spot, I could work down or upstream, casting under overhanging branches for wild and native fish. The fish I caught were from nine to 11 inches, with an occasional one-footer, but, Bob Young landed a 17-inch stream-born brown just before dark in the pool just above the trail from the parking lot.

The biggest wild fish I ever hooked on the Willowemoc, a 14-inch brown, sucked in the small gray nymph I cast into the pool under the bridge to the Covered Bridge Campgrounds. When first hooked the fish jumped, turned, and took off downstream. I had taken 40 small browns and some brooks working my way down to the covered bridge from way above. It had been drizzling rain all morning and *Baetis* flies hatched continuously. You can imagine my surprise when I suddenly found myself connected to this one, shocked out of complacency by its jump upstream—one of those occasions when the fish jumps before you know it's attached to your line. A fat 14-inch fish is a big fish. Biologists tell us that it takes over half a fish's lifetime to grow that big.

The covered bridge under which I hooked this monster wasn't always in its present location. Formerly called the Bendo Bridge and located on the

Willowemoc downstream in Parkston, it was replaced in 1913 by a steel bridge. At the suggestion of Joseph Sherwood, a Livingston Manor resident, it was cut in half and transported nine miles upstream to cross a narrow section of the creek. Today it is surrounded by the Covered Bridge Campground, a privately owned facility. Its official name is the Willowemoc Covered Bridge.

## Upper Beaverkill

I first fished the one mile of public water on the upper Beaverkill just upstream from where it goes under the main road. I had caught a few stocked browns, but was now approaching a wire cable that was strung across the river with a large posted sign hanging from its middle. It was not your normal posted sign. Instead it read "Warning — Poachers Will Be Arrested." This landowner wasn't somebody to fool with! I figured I'd fish up to the sign and then quit. Several yards upstream, I hooked the biggest wild brown I had ever hooked on any section of the river. I hopped and hollered to my friends downstream. That was a big mistake, not because I lost the fish, but because I had alerted the landowner. He came down to the stream as I was netting the 17-inch fish.

He yelled, "Get the hell off of my property, or I'll shoot your ass."

I yelled back, pointing to the midstream sign, "I wasn't over the line."

He yelled back, "That's my neighbor's sign, you're telling me you didn't see my sign on that tree, either you're a lying a—hole or a blind bastard."

Sure enough, having been mesmerized by the larger sign, I had missed his single posted sign on the tree along the bank. I rapidly departed, not because I minded being called a "blind bastard,"

automobile drivers have called me that and worse, but because he was a damn big guy and he was very mad.

Trespassing on posted land is a misdemeanor, a criminal offense, unlike trespassing on unposted land, which is only a minor offense. A criminal offense means jail or a bail bond and you need legal representation before the judge will even hear your case, regardless of how you plea.

Another time I was admonished for encroaching on private lands, my experience had a similar ending. I was fishing an unposted creek and had landed a good-sized trout. Again I hollered and again my hollering alerted the landowner. You'd think I learn! He yelled down,

"Your fishing private water, leave at once."

I yelled back, "I don't keep the fish and I'm using a fly."

He yelled back, "What did you catch it on?"

I yelled back, "A Hair's Ear."

That was all she wrote. For a moment curiosity overcame him, but after hearing the word "nymph" I was admonished with a barrage of curse words intermingled with "You f—-ing nymph fishermen. You're all alike — thoughtless bastards, all of you. Get the hell off my f—-ing land before I call the cops." I found it hard to reconcile his language with his "purist" attitude, but I hurried off anyway.

## The Beaverkill and Willowemoc Today

Today, I rarely fish the upper section of the Willowemoc. Not because the fishing has deteriorated or the land has been posted, but because the easier fishing downstream has grown better. I first learned about the improved fishing on the Beaverkill one afternoon in

*Wading to the tops of one's waders is often necessary to reach rising holdovers
in the Beaverkill's Wagon Tracks Pool.*

1999 when I fished the Wagon Tracks Pool and took six fish just over 12 inches that, while I'm sure they were holdovers, put up a decent fight. The pool got its name from the tracks left by wagons that crossed the river in the old days. In fact, Samuel Darbee was killed when his hay wagon tipped over on him while riding along the banks of the Willowemoc. I never caught six good fish in one evening in the old days. I also caught some nice fish above the old Silver Fox Bar and Grill, now tastefully refurbished into a nice restaurant and motel and renamed the Riverside Café & Lodge.

During an early-morning Hendrickson hatch on an unusually hot spring day in 2002, I had my best day ever on the Willowemoc, catching three browns over 16 inches on three casts in the non-kill section, while an angler downstream from me netted a 24-incher.

Last May, I met two gentlemen who had travel nine hours, one-way, from West Virginia to fish the Beaverkill. They each reported landing two 20-inch fish the day before I arrived. In fact, they did exceptionally well both below the upper no-kill section at Pointer's Bend and on the stretch of the Beaverkill just above the Roscoe Motel where they were staying. Not only did they catch fish in these less restrictive sections, but they also caught big ones, each reporting landing fish over 20 inches in both locations. I doubt if many of the big ones were wild fish, however, because there is no reason to believe that today's big wild fish are any dumber than those of yesteryear. I learned long ago from my friend Val Mihic, who lived on the river, that a streamborn dace, netted during the day and worked carefully at night in the back eddies, was the only way to catch them. Streamers, Rapalas, and even store-bought minnow did not fool them!

I watched the heftier member of the pair fish the pocket-water while I talked to the other who rested on the bank. The resting angler said they had been up before dawn and he, unlike his more gung-ho partner, needed a short break. His friend was an aggressive fisherman, wading waste deep in the high, fast water to plunge nymphs behind every boulder. He would work one boulder and then wade rapidly to the next. He hooked one behind a large boulder in the river's middle but lost it. I had fished that same pocket-water before, but I had cast to it from farther ashore. His position directly over the boulder had given him a better drift. Mine, obviously, whisked by the fish unseen.

This West Virginian was clearly a better fisherman than those who line up in Carin's pool and cast nymphs up and across-stream and then gaze at their strike indicators as their nymphs move slowly downstream. No wonder these two guys caught fish. I am now too old to fish the water into which they feverishly waded, but the fish have to be there for them to catch, a situation that didn't exist when I was younger and able to similarly work the water. These two mountaineers have been visiting the river each May for the past three years and reported having similar luck on each trip.

The Beaverkill has improved not just because it has two no-kill sections, but also because the State includes some larger trout among the thousands of brown trout yearlings it puts into the stream each year. I believe the Roscoe Chamber of Commerce also stocks even bigger fish. Stocking larger trout is greeted with enthusiasm, even if their fight isn't so hot. If they weren't happy, the banks of the major pools in the Beaverkill wouldn't be shoulder to shoulder with fishermen on weekends, and even on some weekdays in May. But there are some holdovers in the no-kill sections that fight reasonably well, and some wild fish also, and that's all it takes to bring me back.

## The Neversink

In the 1970s and 1980s, I often fished the Neversink River above and below the aging hamlet of Woodbourne—the weekend mecca for New York City's Hasidic Jews. (Perhaps the area reminded them of their original home-land in the town of Bobov in Southern Poland, the only mountainous region in their country.) On Fridays, main street would be bustling with activity, but on Saturday afternoons the street would be deserted. Late Saturday night, how-ever, after services, or on Sunday after-noons, it would look like Fifth Avenue.

All of the Neversink River above Claryville has been privately owned since 1882, but the river below the hamlet became a fabled Catskill stream in the early 1900s before the Neversink Reservoir was built, although it was a far different stream than it was in the 1800s. In 1811, lumbermen received financial aid from New York State to clear the river in Sullivan County of boulders, water falls, and other haz-ards, so that lumber could float down the river. Unfortunately, as more lum-ber was cut, the forest shade decreased. As a consequence, the channeled river flowed much faster and became deeper, causing a number of men to drown when trying to raft its turbulent waters and resulting in the suspension of log-ging on the river. Nevertheless, the channeling and widening of the river turned it from a pristine brook trout stream into a fast-flowing brown and rainbow trout river where the fish grew big and fat feeding on insects, min-nows, and crayfish, all of which dra-matically increased following the changes in the river and its environ-ment.

Theodore Gordon tied and fished his famous Quill Gordon on the

Neversink, the fly that set the standard in style and method for the classic Catskill flies still in use today. While fly-fishing historians typically call Gordon and his followers "the fathers of American fly-fishing," they were really the fathers of dry-fly-fishing. Gordon was stimulated by the works of Pennsylvania fishermen who fished with wet flies long before he or C. W. Halford, the British chalk stream angler who set his flies to Gordon to copy in 1885, were born. In fact, Lewis and Clark began their transcontinental trip in 1803 outfitted with flies from a shop on the banks of the Schuylkill near Philadelphia. Gordon spent his summers as a teenager on the banks of the rivers near Carlisle, Pennsylvania, where he became an avid sportsman and collected fly-tying materials from domestic game.

Most of the great New York dry-fly tiers of yesteryear lived along or near the Neversink. They included Edward Hewitt, who bought up five miles along the river and developed his famous Neversink Skater, and Rube Cross, who wrote his two books on fly-tying while living on the river's banks. William Chandler, another famous tier, lived in nearby Liberty, but fished the river regularly. Parker Emery Forte came down from New Hampshire in 1930 and set up the first fly shop in the Catskills in the Village of Neversink.

Before the Neversink dam was completed in 1954, 12 years after seven miles of the river was condemned for the project, large browns were caught in its lower sections. In *McClane's Angling World*, he writes about his friend John Pope, "skimming three big wet flies into the choppers of a waiting trout," on the Neversink where he says the currents were stronger and the water bigger than on the Beaverkill.

Ray Bergman, in his classic work, *Trout*, describes his efforts to take three big fish on a Bridgeville Olive. The three fish weighed a total of 10-1/4 pounds and all were caught in one afternoon's fishing on the Neversink near Oakland. I doubt that this posted section even holds trout today, but if it does it would be because fish moved downstream from the recently established no-kill section in the Neversink Gorge, just above Oakland Valley. I occasionally fish the Neversink below Bridgeville, sometimes with a fly similar to the one Bergman tied and named after this section of the river. Until recently, all I caught was a few small stocked trout and some fairly good sized smallmouth bass. With improved releases from the reservoir, this section now holds significantly more trout and less smallmouth.

The flows from the Neversink reservoir, while small, are fairly steady all year. While most of the river is posted from its headwaters high in the Catskills down to Port Jervis, where it joins the Delaware, the state stocks a small number of unposted sections below the reservoir. The best section, the only no-kill section on the river, is the Neversink Gorge near Thomsonville off Route 17. The fish in this section are wild fish and both brook and brown trout are plentiful. The river bottom in the gorge is composed almost entirely of big, irregular shaped rocks, making it extremely difficult to find a place to put your feet. When the water is moderately high, I can't wade it. In addition, the shore line is infested with mosquitoes.

The biggest trout I have ever caught on the river was a 16-inch wild brown. It was not caught in the gorge, but in a section just above Woodbourne. The river in the five miles below

*The fabled Neversink near Woodbourne.*

the reservoir is like a spring creek. I sometimes hooked a good fish in the pools below riffles, but the distance between riffles is great. It might take two hours to fish six small riffles. I fished it heavily for many years when I was into hiking and exploring as well as fishing. Charles Brooks would have called me a slash-and-run fisherman, a type he mocks in his book *Fishing Yellowstone Waters*. But I was always curious about what I might find just around the next bend or over the next hill. The poet Rainer Marie Rilke put it best when he wrote:

Already my gaze is on the hill, that sunlight one,
up ahead on the path I've scarcely started.
In the same way, what we couldn't grasp, grasps us:
blazingly visible, there in the distance —
and changes us, even if we don't reach it,

into what we, scarcely sensing it, already are;
a gesture signals, answering our gesture...
But we feel only the opposing wind.

I recently bumped into a guy in late September who had hired a guide for a day of fishing on the unposted sections of the Neversink, sections that can be located with the help of a road map, and which are usually fished out of stocked trout in early spring. The angler knew that the river was steeped in Catskill angling history and he wanted to fish it even though he had heard it was a far cry from its early years. He caught nothing, but said he enjoyed the experience anyway. The guide must have served wine, scrimp cocktail, and filet mignon for lunch and been a great companion. The man could have walked the river for free if he wanted to wade in nostalgia!

Some years ago, a story circulated that Bill Kelly, often called Catskill Bill, a fishery's biologist with the New York State Department of Environmental Conservation for 27 years, convinced the state to stock landlocked salmon in the Neversink Reservoir just before his retirement. Nevertheless, all the water below an impassable dam on the upper Neversink has been posted for generations. To access the mouth on reservoir property requires almost a five-mile walk downhill.

The story claims that Kelly had purchased a house on the river just upstream from its mouth and below the dam during the stocking effort. Here is a man who knows how to plan for his retirement! For the past 15 years, 3,000 salmon fry per year have been stocked in its waters, with state biologist Bob Angyal currently studying the results. But did Bill Kelly catch any stream-born fish? Did his bonanza, his "El Dorado," materialize or did he wait, with rod in hand, until his recent death, for a spawning run to develop?

I would bet that many of the salmon fry are eaten by the marauding smallmouth that haunt the river's mouth and for which the reservoir is noted. Some do survive to grow bigger as Mike Zielie has caught several 16-inch landlocks in the Neversink Gorge, miles downstream from the reservoir, and Leonard M. Wright wrote in his 1991 book, *Neversink*, about hooking a 19-incher in the reservoir itself. Unfortunately, he died and any observations he might have made of their spawning efforts below his home on the river died with him.

Bill, an avid fisherman since the age of five, was a great friend of Catskill rivers, challenging dam proposals and reclaiming ponds for brook trout. He died in November of 2000. His presence in the Catskills will be acutely missed and his successful projects will be remembered long after his boondoggle salmon project is forgotten.

## Friends Lost Along the Way

On each of my trips to the Catskills, the surrounding hills and valleys remained pretty much the same, but the area's occupants did not. Time passes, leaving only the faintest of signs, often referred to as universal tracks. Worn mountain tops and abandoned river channels are among these tracks, but human works rarely are. Chief Seattle, a Suquamish Indian, once said, "Every hillside, every valley, every plain and grove, has been hollowed by some sad or happy event in days long vanished." In the 1980s, each time I passed a Catskill resort, I saw that it had closed its doors, no longer providing summer fun for generations of New York City families and both year-round and summer employment for many others.

After the demise of the tanning industry, cleared land in the Catskills became cheap and "country gentlemen" bought up large parcels, for as little as 50¢ an acre, and created estates on the upper sections of Catskill rivers where the brook trout fishing was best. While they were doing so, and the relatively wealthy icons of the fly-fishing world were fishing and tying flies, Jewish immigrants were moving up from the New York City ghettos and buying land as well. During the reign of Alexander the Third in Russia, when the anti-Jewish May laws escalated anti-semitism, more than 1,500,000 Jews immigrated to the United States with three-fourths of them settling in New York City, mostly on the lower East Side. After struggling to survive in the Big Apple's sweatshops, many, with the help of friends and family members, bought small farms in Ulster and Sullivan Counties in the heart of the Catskills. Cash-strapped, their farms were mortgaged to the hilt. They were inexperienced farmers, working soil-poor land under economic hardship, and many needed help from the Jewish Agricultural Society.

To survive economically, many Jewish Catskill families moved into their barns in the summer and rented out their homes to summer guests, selling vegetables to the guests to either cook on the premises or to take back to the city. They had no support from the larger non-Jewish community surrounding them and they were often harassed by local Ku Klux Klan chapters, an organization whose 1868 constitution declared that it would be guided by "chivalry, humanity, mercy, and patriotism." So much for mission statements!

Air conditioning didn't exist when the Jews acquired Catskill land. The only respite from New York City's sweltering summer heat was the cool air in the Catskill Mountains. Excluded from gentile resorts, Jewish workers visited their friends and relatives in the Catskills. These summer boarding homes created the first vacation opportunities for many Jewish people. The word spread and a resort industry was born!

Because local banks would not lend the heavily mortgaged Jewish land owners money, they borrowed it from friends and extended family members and turned their boarding homes into small hotels and, later, into the large resorts that I passed on my way to Catskill rivers in the early 1970s.

Wives and children could stay at the burgeoning Catskill hotels for extended periods while the major breadwinners commuted back and forth on weekends. In the early days, the commute took up to five hours. In its heyday, there were more than 500 hotels, countless bungalows, and numerous children's camps in the Catskills. Many visitors came to the Catskills on trains that no longer operate. In fact, some of the old railroad beds are hidden in vegetation while sections of others have been refurbished as tourist attractions. Many of the trains ran along the sides of rivers and I used to use their former beds to walk up or down a stream.

Many of the comedians I watched on television as a young boy, some of whom had their own television shows, performed in the Catskill Resorts. Eddie Cantor, Sid Caesar, Myron Cohen, Red Buttons, Danny Kaye, and Jerry Lewis appeared regularly. Others, who made me laugh as an adult, were discovered there, such as Orson Bean, Lenny Bruce, "Professor" Irwin Corey, Alan King, and Jackie Mason. Those that make me laugh today, such as Billy Crystal and Bette Midler, also got their start in the Catskills. Countless numbers of less famous funny men and other entertainers made a living performing in the resorts, playing the borscht circuit, as it was referred to in its early days. (Danny Kaye was perhaps the first "toomler," or all-around entertainer and creator of tumult, to perform in the Catskill resorts.)

The airplane's invention changed the Catskills forever, followed by the cruise ships that provided recreational services rivaling those of the Catskill resorts, but with island hops thrown in. Over a relatively short period of time the number of hotels dwindled from 500 to less than 12. The largest resort industry in the United States simply vanished. The smaller hotels were abandoned and deteriorated while the larger ones were bought up by nonprofit organizations. The bigger survivors now serve the convention trade and the smaller survivors cater to special interest groups, like the Hasidic Jews.

The resorts rescued the Catskills from bankruptcy following the closure of the tanneries in the late 1800s. Now the Catskills were bankrupt again since the influx of the nonprofit organizations did nothing to improve the local economy. The corner regulars I waved at and the luncheonettes I stopped at, where the owners greeted me with a handshake, gradually disappeared. It became a lonely commute.

## The Tanneries

Before the Catskills became a vacation center they were a tanning center, and it was this industry that decimated the forests of hemlock trees and changed Catskill streams forever. Without trees the streambeds eroded and the trout suffered. The bark of the hemlock tree was a source of tannin, a substance used in leather production. Before the tanneries, about 27% of the trees in the Catskill forests were Hemlocks, trees that grow primarily along streambeds. Those forests in regions interlaced with streams would have even more hemlocks—up to 40% of the trees. After a tree was cut, it was stripped of its bark up to its first branch, the easiest bark to remove, and left to rot on the ground. The effort required to remove bark from above the first branch was greater than the effort required to cut down another tree and strip its lower bark. The bark from the trees was carted to the tannery, located along the rivers, where the hides were waiting for tanning.

Tanning was a dirty, arduous job and each of its steps contributed to a stream's pollution. First, each animal skin, typically shipped from South America and then carted to the Catskills, required washing in hot water for about 30 hours. Keeping the water hot required cutting down other trees for cord wood. Second, there was the long process of further soaking each skin in a lye-water solution to loosen the hair so it could be more easily scraped off. This process took about a year, with discarded solutions either dumped directly into a stream or seeping into it. Third, and the most disastrous for a stream, the de-haired hide was then tanned by immersing it in a bath of hemlock bark, produced by grinding the bark in a bark mill as it was mixed with water from a stream. Finally, the hide was dried and finished until it looked like leather.

Catskill tanneries supplied most of the saddles used in the Civil War. The largest tannery in the Catskills was located at De Bruce where Mongaup Creek joins the Willowemoc. Thirty-thousand acres of trees were cut to produce the 60,000 hides that were tanned annually. When the hemlocks were gone, the tanners turned to oak. When the oaks were gone, the tanning industry collapsed, as did the region's prosperity. As the forest re-grew, lumbering for local use was replaced by large-scale cutting for the furniture industry.

## The Catskill Stream Club

While the Jewish immigrants were running their hotels, a number of wealthy Catskill landowners, whose ancestors had bought property along the upper sections of Catskill streams to establish preserves for their fishing and hunting pleasure, sold their lands to other groups who turned them into fishing clubs, called the Catskill Stream Clubs by outsiders. The riverfront property owned by each club ranged from one-and-one-half miles to seven

*The famous Junction Pool.*

miles. Clubs on the upper Beaverkill included the Balsam Lake Club, the Beaverkill Trout Club, The Big Bend Club, and the Clear Lake Club. On the Neversink, there was even a women's club—the Women's Fly Fishers Club. These clubs still own close to 25% of river property in the Catskills, but their land is concentrated, as is the remaining estate property, on the upper portions of the Beaverkill and the Neversink.

### Accommodations and Other Activities

Anglers who enjoy resorts can stay at the Huff House (800-243-4567), located near Roscoe. The Inn is a typical Catskill resort. The Huff House has 47 rooms, a heated pool, a spring-fed trout pond, and a nine-hole golf course. The Tennanah Lake Lodge, Golf and Country Club, a former resort near Roscoe, is now closed and the lodge itself is owned by The Foundation for a Course in Miracles. Maybe if I enrolled in their course, I could catch a 20-inch wild fish in the Beaverkill!

Other anglers may prefer to stay and dine at The Guest House (845-439-4000), or at the De Bruce County Inn (845-439-4844), rated as one of the top 50 inns in America, located on the banks of the upper Willowemoc off De Bruce Road (County Road 82), or the Beaverkill Valley Inn at Lew Beach (845-439-4884), where guests can fish a mile of private water, play tennis, or swim in an indoor pool. This nineteenth-century inn—one of the loveliest inns I have seen—is the most expensive inn in the Catskills. Saturday night dinner, for example, costs around $33.

The owners of the Reynolds House Inn and Motel (607-498- 4422) claim it is the oldest bed and breakfast in the country. It features kitchenettes in the motel rooms, caters to fishermen, and is located in the village of Roscoe, a short walk up the street to the Little Store, the two full service fly shops, and down the street to the Roscoe Diner. Those preferring to dine at their motel can choose either the Rockland House (607-498-4772) or the Red Rose Motel

*Willowemoc Creek's largest browns dwell in the waters just below
the bridge to the Catskill Fly Fishing Museum.*

and Restaurant (607-498-5525). Most out-of-state anglers stay at the Roscoe Motel, located at the Junction Pool, owned by George and Debra Kinne.

The Kinnes also operate the Baxter House Bed & Breakfast (607-498-5220), which caters to anglers, and is located right on the river off Old Route 17. There are at least four other bed and breakfast inns near the two rivers. Three are located just south of Livingston Manor on Shandelee Road—Huber's Shandelee Lake Farm (845-439-5293), the Mountain View Inn (845-439-5070), and The Magical Land of Oz (845-439-3418), the latter being very inexpensive and rustic, almost dorm-like, with a lake in which guests can swim. A forth inn, the Campbell Inn, is located south of Roscoe on Tennanah Road.

For those preferring a more rustic atmosphere, Creekside Cabins (607-498-5873) rents seven efficiency cabins on the Willowemoc near Livingston Manor. Livingston Manor was named for Edward Livingston, nephew of Chancellor Livingston, discussed in Chapter Seven, who owned thousands of acres in the Catskills. Also in Livingston Manor, is the Willowemoc

Motel, right on the river on De Bruce Road and across and slightly downstream from the Fur, Fin, and Feather Sports Shop (845-439-4476).

There are a number of campgrounds to choose from on or near the Beaverkill. Anglers planing to fish the no-kill section just below Roscoe can stay at either the Roscoe Campsite (607-498-5264) or the Twin Island Campsite (845-498-5326). Those anglers fishing the no-kill section at Horton can stay either at the Butternut Grove Campgrounds (607-498-4224), right on the river, or at the Russell Brook Campsite (607-498-5416) at Cooks Falls, about a mile from the river, where on-site trailers can be rented. Anglers desiring a somewhat different experience for their families can stay at Merrill's Farm Vacations (607-498-4212), an inn in Horton featuring farm vacations and rooms and meals by the day or week.

Campers planning to fish the mile stretch of public water on the upper Beaverkill at Lew Beach, where the Wulff School of Fly Fishing (845-439-4060) is located, can stay at either of two state campgrounds, the Beaverkill Campsite and Covered Bridge

(845-439-4233), below Lew Beach, or the Little Pond Campsite (845-439-5480), above Lew Beach.

Anglers fishing the upper Willowemoc, can stay at one of several campgrounds off De Bruce Road that parallels the Willowemoc River. Closest to Livingston Manor is the Covered Bridge Campsite (845-439-5093). Further up the road, seven miles northeast of De Bruce, is the Mongaup Pond State Campground (800-436-CAMP) at the source of Mongaup Creek. Last, is the Long Pond Lean-To (845-439-5480), a state campground about 14 miles above Livingston Manor. Those choosing to fish the river above De Bruce can camp at the Willowemoc Campgrounds (845-439-4250) on Route 82, now called Willowemoc Road. Those who enjoy lakes can camp at the Hunter Lake Campground (845-292-3629) on spring-fed Hunter Lake, just south of De Bruce, where family members can fish, swim, and boat.

I stay at the Riverside Café and Lodge (607-498-5305) in Horton, operated by Tammy Sherwood with the help of her mother who lives next door. Tammy is a graduate of the Culinary Institute of America who formerly worked at the Beaverkill Valley Inn.

There are seven antique stores, three gift shops, and a railroad museum in the general area, but there is not much to do in the evening in the Beaverkill Valley, except dinner and bed. In Roscoe, anglers used to gather to swap stories and share an excellent meal at the Antrim Lodge, but it is now closed and the popular Roscoe Dinner is a poor substitute.

The Catskill Fly Fishing Center and Museum (845-439-4810), located on Old Route 17 between Livingston Manor and Roscoe, affords anglers the opportunity to fish on one of the Willowemoc's no-kill sections and to take a break between hatches and enjoy exhibits exploring the history, art, and science of fly-fishing, including a look at Lee Wulff's fly tying desk every Saturday from opening day to October, where a guest fly tier demonstrates tying techniques. Children from eight to 18 can stay at the center for the weekend and learn the basic of fly-fishing, fly tying, and river ecology. Girls and boys stay in separate bunk houses and enjoy rain or shine events, wholesome meals, and a full schedule of interesting activities.

There are 40 miles of recreational trails, most of which originated as old roads, but few offer majestic views. Unlike the Northern Catskills, the area near Livingston Manor and Roscoe does not include a named summit. While generally hilly, the majority of hills in the Willowemoc-Long Pond Wild Forest are less than 3,000 feet in height and vary in elevation from one another no more than 1,000 feet. The terrain varies from long, steep-sided ridges to lower elevation wetlands, lakes, and ponds.

The only cultural activity in the area is a sunset concert series held during August at the Shandelee Musical Festival Pavilion (845-439-3227), near Livingston Manor, but typically there are no more than five performances. The group also tries to arrange for one Broadway play. In 1994, a not-for-profit organization, the Institute for Development of Entertainment Arts, was founded in an effort to re-develop the Catskills as a cultural and entertainment center. Perhaps there will be more evening activities in future years.

CHAPTER FIVE

# Small Catskill Streams
## *Where Trout Fishing Began*

When I first moved to the Shawangunk Mountains in Ulster County, New York, I had no idea which of the numerous streams in the immediate area would hold native trout. I tried them all, with many having unusual names, like Coxing Kill, a native American name for "near a high place," Dwarr Kill, the Dutch word for "across," and Fantine Kill, Dutch for "one with rapids." From the Shawangunk Valley, I walked up the Verkeendear Kill, named after an early Dutch settler, and worked my way down the Kleine Kill, meaning "little brook." From the Rondout Valley, I fished up the Kripplebush Creek, and near the lower Esopus I fished the Tongore Kill, named after an Esopus Indian Chief. Two with common names, like the Bear Kill and the Bear Kill West Branch were named, not after the Black Bears that inhabit the Catskills, but after an early settler named Baehr. Some of these little brook trout streams were good, but most were not, and I rarely fished any of them again.

### Streams in the Rondout Valley

After several seasons of exploration, I concentrated my efforts on the Rondout Creek, originally known as the Little Esopus, in Rondout Valley and on several of its tributaries. The valley is bordered on the east by the Shawangunk Mountains, or Gunks, as they are affectionately called by the rock climbers who come from all over the East to scale their cliff faces. The Gunks are much older than the Catskills, being a conglomeration of limestone and quartz. Their name, created from a combination of native American words, means either "at the hillsides" or "at the south." Their rocks are white and shine in the sun, contrasting wonderfully with the mountain laurel and wild rhododendron that grow throughout the forests. Long before my time, rocks for the world famous Esopus Wheel Stones were quarried in the Gunks. On the west the valley is bordered by the Catskills, where the even more famous Catskill Bluestones were excavated, stones that don't get slippery when wet, and that can still be walked upon in towns throughout the world.

I fished the Rondout in the riffled sections near towns where the original Dutch, German, and French settlers kept the original Native American names for the spots where they built their homes. The first town downstream of Ellenville is Napanoch, a town whose name means "land overflowed with water," an appropriate name, not only because the Sandberg Creek joins the Rondout at the town, but because several other creeks flow nearby. Lackawack, an early settlement on the Rondout above Napanoch, means "the fork of a river." Warwarasing, the next town downstream from Napanoch, means "a rapid stream." Kerhonkson, means "shallow water," an appropriate name as the river flows over a long rock shelf behind the town.

The tributaries I fished were the Sandberg Creek, Rochester Creek, Mill Brook, and Vernooy Kill. These streams, though stocked, contained wild fish in pleasant stream environments and an occasional wild brown or native brook trout can still be caught in them today. I first fished the Sandberg Creek above Ellenville where the state had a fisherman's easement off Zarobchick Road. Later, I fished in a section off Mc Dole Road. It was a winding wooded section, with good riffles and runs, deep

holes, and numerous fallen trees, both in midstream and along its banks, that provided cover for wild fish. Trees that lay across the creek had to be climbed over or walked around, activities that discouraged the casual fisherman. Many flies were lost to the trees or to sunken logs. The fly had to float right along a fallen tree, often getting hung up in a branch before a well-hidden trout could rise up to seize it.

### The Rochester Creek

The Rochester Creek, where I spent most of my time, is stocked near its mouth at the Rondout Creek and at its junction with Mill Brook, about a mile above the Rondout. The Mill Creek is a lazy, meandering creek flowing mostly through farm land. To long-time valley residents these two creeks go by different names. Rochester Creek is the Mettacahonts and Mill Creek is the Mombaccus. But even some residents, map makers, and historians confused the names of these two creeks and the brooks that feed them. Originally, the Rochester was a small book that entered the Beaver Dam Brook from the east before it joined the Mettacahonts at the hamlet of Liebardt.

The Mettacahonts drains the northwest slopes of Mombaccus Mountain. The Mombaccus drains the highlands southeast of Mt. Sampson, but was named after the hamlet of Mombaccus through which it flows on its way to join the Mettacahonts at Mill Hook. In the early 1700s, the Mombaccus, being primarily a valley stream, was a perfect stream for grist mills and most of its ease ways were granted to mill owners, causing it to eventually become known as Mill Brook. The names of these mill owners are familiar to most residents who live in the Rondout Valley—

Dewitt, Hornbeck, Oosterhoudt, VanWagnen, Vernooy, Quick, Schoonmaker, and Westbrock. In the 1800s, new mills, grist and lumber, replaced the old grist mills, but the names of their owners are less well known.

Today, the Rochester Creek above Mill Hook contains more wild browns than any river in the Catskills. The fish caught on a fly run small, between eight and 11 inches, but the river flows first among chestnuts, maples and oaks, and, then, among the pines and hemlocks that grow along the steep cliffs, from which several small tributaries flow that hide native brook trout. One tributary's waters tumble more than 20 feet over a ledge into the creek, its midst usually creating a small rainbow for me to admire. I always expected to see a bobcat or lynx stopping to take a drink in this primitive setting, but I never did. Perhaps one heard me coming and moved on. I like to think so even though very few Bobcats remain in the Catskills. The tall hemlocks in the creek's middle sections form a canopy 100 feet from the valley floor. Rays from the sun angle through the canopy and diffuse into a pattern of shadow and light on the creek's rocks and pools that would humble any artist creating a mosaic. I like to put my head back and stare up at the tops of these tall trees, knowing that no man has ever touched their uppermost needles, but when the wind blows their tops and then swoops down to chill my face, I feel I have touched them.

Further up the mountain, the shade from the trees is so dense, that I feel compelled to turn back, realizing I am a foreigner and that other species own the right to walk here. Early writers talk about how the dark Catskill forests, the catalyst for tales of witches and goblins, became open and airy when the hemlocks were replaced by deciduous trees. But one ray of sunlight dissolves the darkness and the spooky feeling along with it, and I keep going up the stream. On each trip to the creek, I leave behind me the worries that steal my peace and open myself to the healing that, before each day is over, fills my mind with new aspirations.

The Rochester Creek, with its copper-colored waters, taught me one fascinating fact about wild trout. Once I learned this secret, I was rarely skunked on a visit to the creek's cascading waters. In the early spring, I would cast small streamers into the creek's undercut banks and beneath its fallen trees. I kept a log that recorded the specific streamer on which I had fooled each fish and the exact spot in the river where it had been fooled. By spot, I mean a single fish lie. If I had fooled a fish on a Mickey Finn, a red and yellow bucktail first tied by Pennsylvania angler John Allen Knight, I could cast a Mickey Finn 15 times into the spot and not catch the fish I had returned there earlier in the week. Had it been caught? Had it left? Brown trout can travel quite far up and down creeks. Neither! After resting the spot, I would switch to another streamer and bang, fish on!

The stream below Mill Hook contains stocked trout, but streamborn ones also can be caught. I once took Dave Whitaker, an angler unfamiliar with the creek, to a stretch several hundred yards below the falls at Mill Hook. As we walked into the woods, a flock of turkey buzzards swooped through the trees, startling us as they flew noisily over our heads. We had to stop under trumpet vines that had worked their way up the trees along the river, growing thick at the tree's top, hogging the sun's rays, and eventually killing the host tree.

When we entered the creek, Dave selected a black Woolly Worm and proceeded to work it along the banks. The Woolly Worm was first tied on large hooks to fool bass. Later it was tied in smaller sizes, quickly becoming a favorite of trout fishermen. It had been drizzling since we arrived and when it started to rain harder, the water began to discolor rapidly. Dave quickly cast his fly up into the cloudy water that was flowing down to him. Instantly, his rod bent and a fish shot out of the water. He landed a fat 14-inch brown with beautiful coloration, a fish to sit and admire, but he quickly returned it. After the creek became coffee brown, we quit for the day. On our ride home, Dave thanked me for taking him to the stream because the brown was the biggest wild fish he had hooked in several years in spite of having access to private waters on the Wappinger Creek, a good Dutchess County trout stream.

Ray Bergman writes that trout can be taken on streamers just as the stream waters discolor. He learned this fact when fishing a creek on which saw mills still operated. Immediately following the initial discharge from a mill, which put down rising fish, Bergman would switch from a dry fly to a streamer and hook fish, but once the mill was in full swing, and the water completely discolored, he caught nothing. In early April I have caught 18-inch browns in the Rondout Creek itself on weighted streamers, but, unlike Dave on his one trip, I have never taken a 14-inch wild brown in any of the Rondout's major feeder creeks. I have taken them elsewhere, however, and the situation reminds me of William Humphrey's classic short

story, "My Moby Dick," which captured the dreams of fishermen everywhere.

## My Moby Dicks

I park along the road, crawl under a farmer's fence, cross his fields, and after a brief hike through thorny weeds and wild raspberries, I am at the mouth of a little brook that enters the Rondout after flowing down from the Shawangunk Mountains. When I first discovered this creek in 1972, it contained a nice bank run, a brief spiraling riffle, a three-foot-deep pool below the riffle, followed by another riffle along an undercut bank, and a deep, cool pool where it joined the Rondout Creek. Each year, however, high spring flows change its shape. As a result, the small section just above the mouth might not be attractive to fish in any given year. I'm talking no more than 25 yards here! What never changed, however, was the little creek's actual mouth. On each side of the creek was an old stone bridge abutment. Many of the rocks from the abutment fell into the creek over the years, making the bottom rocky when normally it would be fine gravel and sand. It stayed that way from year to year because the high waters of the Rondout washed it free of sand and debris. The logs that occasionally became affixed to the downstream abutment just made it more attractive to the trout.

In this 25-yard section, large browns from the Rondout, a marginal trout stream in this section, entered the creek to feed on its hatches, its large minnow life, its abundant crayfish, and to escape the summer heat. Nevertheless, in spite of my knowledge of its secrets, I never caught any of the Moby Dicks that moved into this water. I did catch several about 17

*The falls on the Rondout Valley's Vernooy Kill creates a wild brook trout fishery up to its headwaters.*

inches, but I never caught any of the heart stoppers.

The Moby Dicks stayed in the deep, cool pool at the actual mouth where I could not cast to them. The pool was too deep to wade, as was the river in front of it, and the large abutments prevented me from getting into the proper casting position. Today, if I were of the mind to do so, I could probably cast to the big fish, if they still went there, by anchoring a float tube in the main river. But after a long float from the put-in spot, there might be no hatch in progress and no fish actively

feeding. These big fish couldn't be fooled by a streamer because the water in the pool is still and crystal clear.

## The Vernooy Kill

When I first fished the Vernooy Kill, located just south of Ellenville, the best section, located between Brownsville and Pottersville, was posted by a rod and gun club, forcing me to fish the headwaters above Pottersville, located on State Forest Preserve Land. In the late 1990s, the rod and gun club sold their land to a conservation group that denoted it to the state in 2002. Now, except for a short stretch about a mile above the mouth, the river can be fished all the way to its headwaters. Because of a waterfall in its lower stretch, the upper creek is a stronghold for native brook trout and is easily accessed by a road that parallels its scenic length.

I enjoyed hiking into this upper section because it gave me access to two different streams on the same mile-and-a-half journey. Off Upper Cherrytown Road, about three miles above the road's junction with Baker and Wright Roads, are blue trail markers on the road's west side. They mark the beginning of a trail to Vernooy Falls. The trail is an abandoned town road where the hiker first crosses a stepping-stone-sized creek and than crosses the upper Mill Brook on a snowmobile bridge. The trail then ascends a ridge, levels out to round a hill, passes by a road that forks left, and makes a small descent to the Vernooy Kill at Vernooy Falls. The Vernooy Kill is named after Cornelius Vernooy who imported machinery from Holland to start the area's first grist mill. The rock wall of a former mill extends along the east bank of the stream by the falls. Both above and below the falls, the stream tumbles over boulders, creating pockets for small wild trout.

If I was in the mood for a mountain drive, and the roads were dry, I drove northeast on Sundown Road and took Trails End Road to Mountain Road, a gravel road that skirts the edges of Balsam Swamp, the headwaters of the Vernooy Kill, about a half mile above the falls. Here the road changes its name to Spencer Road, as it goes along the base of Samson Mountain, and eventually ends on the East Branch of the Rondout Creek at Greenville, certainly not the easiest way to get to the creek, but one where I didn't have to retrace my steps.

## Upper Rondout Creek

The West Branch of the Rondout Creek, the third stream to rise in the Slide Mountain massif, originates between Rocky and Balsam Cap Mountains. It flows south between Lone, Table, and Peekamoose Mountains, joins a stream flowing out of Peekamoose Lake, and swells through the hamlet of Bull Run until joined by the smaller East Branch at Sundown. The stream is breathtaking. None like it exists in the Catskills. John Burroughs, the great naturalist, wrote, "If I were a trout, I should ascend every stream until I found the Rondout." Contributing to its charm are granite-bottomed runs with overhanging hemlocks, struggling to stay rooted to its mossy cliffs, ferns along its banks, with tangled tree roots below, large, flat boulders abutting deep pools, and shallow riffles interspersed with clumps of long-stemmed grasses.

In its upper sections, the cliffs drip with heavy moisture and the sunlight struggles for existence. An ever-present mist brings out the deep colors of the cliffs and overhanging trees—the moss is greener and the browns appear black, ominous, and foreboding. Walking upstream, cool, brisk air strikes your face, but then warmth from air trapped in crevices or under the canopy of bushes mixes with it. It is a place not just to fish, but a place to sit on a rock and to feel and to think more deeply. It is not a place where, quoting native American writer Jane Sequichie Hifler, "We forget and think we are all there is," but rather a place to penetrate more deeply into the mysteries of life.

Angling writer Ross Kushner emphasizes that campers occupy its riverbanks, especially on weekends, but few camp on the river before school closes for the summer. On hot summer weekends, campers line the river to cool their feet while others swing from a rope out over the water and drop into the Blue Hole, where I once landed a 15-inch wild brown.

Huge Seeforellen browns from the Rondout Reservoir used to run up the creek to spawn in the fall after the season was closed. During the season, a 15-pounder was caught near the mouth on a streamer. The fish was stocked in 1986 and caught in 1992. The largest recorded brown caught in the reservoir was 19 pounds, 36-plus inches, taken in 1995 by a 15-year-old boy. Where could he go from there? A 20-pound, 33-inch brown, netted in the Rondout, hangs over the reception desk at the Region 3 office of the New York State Department of Environmental Conservation.

Seeforellen browns are no longer stocked in the reservoir, but those that are stocked, as well as the wild Seeforellen that remain, grow to respectable sizes and are often caught in the fall near the mouth of the Rondout and in Sugarbush Creek that enters the Rondout Creek near its mouth at the reservoir.

*Bob Young working a run on Upper Rondout Creek.*

### The Lower Rondout Creek

I first fished the lower Rondout at Alligerville. It is a much bigger stream in the valley, actually it's a river. I had taken a road from my home that ascends the Shawankunks, passes the entrance to famous Lake Mohonk Mountain House, descends into the Rondout Valley—providing a marvelous view of the Catskills—and passes over the river at Alligerville. From the road I spotted a nice looking riffle just above the bridge and decided to try it. I threw a Mickey Finn into the river and worked it downstream. As soon as it floated behind a midstream boulder, I was into a good fish. When it jumped, I realized it was a smallmouth. It measured 17 inches. Catching my first fish from an unknown river was extremely satisfying, even thought it wasn't a trout, and I went home excited by my discovery.

Alligerville was an old Delaware and Hudson Canal town, known for its taverns and Irish brawls. At one time, the canal, known as the D&H Canal, ran through the valley and past the town. The D&H Canal was the brainchild of Maurice and William Wurts, namesakes of the Town of Wurtsboro, who, along with other mine owners, wanted to transport coal from their extensive coal fields in northeastern Pennsylvania to New York City. Work began on the canal in 1823, it opened in 1828, and it was enlarged in 1842 and again in 1851.

By hand, with the help of draft horses, Irish immigrants cleared the land, dug out the 108-mile-long pit, and constructed 109 locks, 15 aqueducts, and 14 boat basins, including the Rondout Basin in Kingston where the coal was barged to New York City. The canal wound an awkward but practical line from Honesdale, Pennsylvania, southeast along the Lackawaxen River, over the Roebling Bridge across the Delaware river, and down along the Delaware to Port Jervis before working its way northeast up the Rondout Valley along the Bashakill and Rondout Creek.

The canal was open each year from the spring through the early winter. To make ends meet, boat owners, who worked with a single vessel, needed one load each week to make a profit. Consequently, their mules and horses towed their boats while walking along the towpath 18 hours a day, six days a week, in order to travel from one end of the canal to the other. Many of the boatmen were assisted by orphans they took in who earned less than $2 a week and who were paid only at the end of the season. The lads walked the whole way with the horses each week and rested only on Sunday. The boatmen hoped the boys would tire and run away toward the end of the season so they wouldn't have to pay them. The last load of coal went through the canal in 1878 after which it was sold to a Kingston-based steamship company and later abandoned in favor of the railroads.

Inspired by my own writing, I returned last April to fish the head of the pool above the bridge at Alligerville. Casting a bead-headed black Woolly Bugger upstream, using a full sinking line, and letting it drift back down stream like a dislodged Hellgrammite, I caught three smallmouth, one about 12 inches and the other two about 14, big smallmouth for a Catskill stream.

## Woodland Creek

In the late 1970s and early 1980s, when the Esopus was too high to comfortably fish, I went to the Woodland Creek

that feeds the Esopus just above Phoenicia. The Woodland Valley is one of the Catskill's deepest valleys and it penetrates into the area's most remote peeks. Its earlier name, Snyder's Hollow, was more fitting. The terrain is rugged, with interesting homesteads along the road and two lively brook trout streams that run under it— Panther Kill and Dougherty Brook. Sometimes I fished it from the mouth up, trying to visualize Samson's Tannery in operation while I worked my way up to where a second tannery used to be located, about a mile-and-a-half upstream. It was later converted to a hoop-making factory and I tried to imagine its workers sweating inside.

In early spring, the morning sun's reflection bronzes the windows of the homes along the river. The smoke from their wood burning stoves swirls upwards into the sky and I wish I was inside cozily sharing a coffee with the residents. But when the water sings as it flows swiftly by me and I see the shafts of sunlight, caught in the dew, light up each blade of grass and splash color against the trunk of every riverside tree, I realize that cold and solitude are my friends and that the friendship of the residents is not needed. As I wade and cast beside the frosted bank grasses, ablaze like gems, I clean my mind of the trash that I have inadvertently stashed there, my mind is set adrift, and things out of order fall into place. Sitting by a warm fire is a nice idea, but it is a poor substitute.

A two-mile, fly-fishing-only, stretch of the Woodland Creek has been stocked for more than forty years with browns, some over 12 inches, by the Woodland Valley Fly Fishers, a private group. I learned of the group when I found a note under my car's windshield wipers asking for a contribution to support their stocking activities. I sent them ten bucks and received in return a thank-you note, written on Time Incorporated letterhead, and a little yellow tag shaped like a trout to hang over my rearview mirror. Out of curiosity, I used to check each parked car to see if a little yellow trout was visible through the windshield. None ever were.

I learned later that Paul O'Neil, a summer resident of the creek, and his wife, stocked the creek themselves and printed up the notes, requesting contributions to help reimburse them for their costs. Paul had taken over this responsibility from Fred Muehleck, another summer resident who had made arrangements with landowners for fishing rights along the stream. Entrepreneurship knows no bounds! Paul's son, Mike, continues the stock-ing program today.

Like the Woodland Creek, two of the most highly touted Catskill streams in the early 1900s were two feeder creeks to the Esopus, the Bush Kill and Bakeman Kill, whose lower reaches no longer exist and whose upper reaches have been reduced to a trickle. Both entered the Esopus near West Shokan, a stretch of the riverbed that now lies under the Ashokan Reservoir. The best of the two, the Bush Kill, in Watson Hallow, with six feeder creeks, provided brook trout for the hiking angler in spite of the five sawmills, two stave mills, and large tannery located along its banks. Two small private sporting clubs, the Maltby Valley Falls Club and The Moon Haw Club, were located along Maltby Hollow Brook, a feeder stream to the Bush Kill. Those anglers unable or uninterested in joining the clubs, stayed at the Watson Hollow Inn located on the kill. Due to considerable fishing pressure, the state stocked over 30,000 brook trout in the Bush Kill in 1899.

For all practical purposes, brook trout no longer live in the Bushkill. The last stream study to find brook trout in this creek or in its four lower tributaries was completed in 1936. An electrofishing study of four sections of the stream in 1994 revealed only one brook

*Woodland Creek.*

56

WENDY NEEFUS

*Art Flick at his tying bench in the 1970s.*

residents, and they renamed the little hamlet after the family.

## Northeastern Streams Where Catskill Fishing Began

Twenty years ago, I fished for wild trout in four Greene County streams. They were the Schoharie, a north flowing river, its two upper tributaries the East and West Kills, and a lower tributary, the Batavia Kill, which enters the river above Prattsville. Each time I fished the East Kill, I used to enjoy visualizing George and Evaline Showers operating their tavern near the headwaters of the creek in the late 1890s. The town line passed through the tavern's center, enabling patrons to dance on the East Jewett side, which was a dry township, and to drink on the Hunter side. Before George operated the tavern, he managed the family farm near Tannersville and worked at a saw mill in Phoenicia, as did some of his neighbors, walking the 36-mile round-trip from his home to the mill every other day and staying at the mill's bunk house in between.

Art Flick's studies of river life that resulted in his *Streamside Guide to Naturals and their Artificials* included samples from the Schoharie. Art was known as The Laird of the West Kill, because of the tavern/guest house he operated on this feeder to the Schoharie. Ray Bergman and Preston Jennings both stayed at Flick's Westkill Tavern. Art took it over from his father in 1934 and operated it until he retired in 1960.

Long before fishermen came to the Westkill tavern, anglers fished Greene County streams. The Village of Catskill, first settled in 1640, was the main gateway to the mountains directly west of the village, the first mountains to be considered Catskill

trout, at the stream's junction with Kanape Brook, way upstream at its headwaters, and it was only four inches long. Yet, close to 80 brown trout were captured at this same section, ranging in size from two inches to ten inches, suggesting that the brown trout have crowded out the brook trout, even in the higher elevations of Catskill streams.

Northwest of the Woodland Valley is a much bigger Bush Kill, flowing through the hamlets of Fleischmann and Arkville in the northwestern Catskills. Charles F. Fleischmann, a gin maker from Cincinnati, stayed at Griffin's Corners, perhaps at the inn operated by O. Vermilya, noted for catering to those of German ancestry, who advertised, "Trout streams near at hand." He was so impressed with the area that he built an estate there in 1883 and visited it regularly using his own private railroad. He and his immediate relatives, who often joined him there, were very generous to local

*Pocket water on the Schoharie below its junction with the East Kill.*

Mountains. As many as 50 steamships cruised up and down the Hudson River between New York City and Albany in the early 1800s and Catskill Landing was their primary unloading spot. The Catskill Mountain House, the subject of many painting by artists of the Hudson River School, opened in 1824. The nation's first mountain house stood high on a cliff ledge overlooking Kaaterskill Cove at Pine Orchard, standing as a symbol of the new nation's wealth and cultural ambitions.

Because the Kaaterskill was the closest stream to the Mountain House, it was the first inland Catskill creek fished by traveling anglers. Others who wet a line in the local streams stayed in the boarding houses in the Village of Catskill and fished the lower Kaaterskill south of where it joins the Kattskill (Catskill Creek) or they fished the Kattskill itself, a valley stream that originates in a swamp near Franklinton in Schoharie County. The creek is now a marginal fishery, relying primarily upon stocked fish and put and take fishing.

Local creeks were well known, having been depicted by many artists. Thomas Cole did an oil painting of Kattskill Creek in 1833 and William H. Bartlett did an engraving of Katterskill Falls in 1840, the highest water falls in New York State, falling 260 feet in two steps of 175 feet and 85 feet. When tourists first came, locals dammed the creek at the top of the falls and when a significant number had gathered at the prime viewing sites, they would release the water for a fee.

When the Stoney Clove Railroad laid tracks between the towns of Phoenicia and Hunter in 1880, linking the Esopus and Schoharie Valleys, the trickle of visitors to the region became a torrent. The 1890 census revealed 900 boarding houses in Hunter alone, a town whose population swelled from 30,000 in the winter to 70,000 in the summer. Today less than 600 people are residents of Hunter.

To attract fishermen, merchants enlisted the services of local hatcheries to help replenish the local streams. In 1880, A. W. Marks put close to 200,000 brook trout from his Prattsville hatchery into selected Greene County streams. In 1886, the state stocked European brown trout, a trout species more tolerant of polluted water than brook trout, but still continued to stock hundreds of thousands of brook trout, supplemented by selective private stocking of brook trout, the species preferred by visiting fishermen. Anglers could fish for these stocked trout, as well as for the few remaining natives, only during July and August, Greene County's fishing season at the time.

The Schoharie Valley was the most heavily timbered of the valleys in the Catskills and as a result, the Schoharie River below the Village of Hunter now flows through fields and scrub bushes rather than through woods. The same had been true for the West Kill, but Art Flick and his friends planted willows along the river to help correct the condition. The Schoharie would become very warm in the summer, trout would seek refuge elsewhere, and fishermen would move to other rivers. But, surprisingly, there were often good fish in the river in the fall. Nevertheless, the river was always at risk, but the lowering of its winter water by a ski lodge put it over the edge.

In the 1980s Hunter Mountain Ski Resort increased its snow-making capacity and began to make 300 inches of snow each year by pumping water directly from the Schoharie River. Water levels in the Schoharie got so low during the winter months that most of the insect life perished. The river is still stocked each spring, but the fish are rapidly caught and little food exists to help the few remaining survivors to grow. I hope the river spirits who look after Art Flick keep secret from him the river's demise.

## The Saw Kill and Beaver Kill

South of the Kaaterskill is the Platte Kill, a Dutch word meaning "a smooth flowing stream," and the Saw Kill. Today, both these Ulster County streams give up only stocked fish, but in the early 1800s the Saw Kill and the Beaver Kill, a small feeder to the Esopus that flows west of the village of Woodstock, were major trout streams. Ulster County anglers living near Kingston, or Manhattan anglers arriving there by steamship, could travel by stagecoach to Woodstock and stay at village inns that had been serving guests since 1789.

James Pierce, in his *Memoir in the Catskill Mountains*, published in 1823, mentions that 500 trout per day could be caught in two tributaries to the Saw Kill—the Mink Hollow and Silver Hollow books, the later already famed as a Tory hideout during the Revolutionary War. While I am sure that Mr. Pierce didn't invent the tall-tale, his exaggeration ranks high on the list. Five hundred trout per day is more than a fish a minute in an eight-hour day! No one catches a fish a minute all day long, even in the good ole days. Today, with roads and summer homes in their water drainage, the Mink and Silver Hollow Brooks are little more than trickling cascades of water.

Later, Charles Lanman, in *Adventures in the Wilds of the United States of American and the British Area Providences*, described, in 1856, the excellent fishing in the upper Saw Kill, a creek he called Sweetwater Brook. The early Dutch settlers first called the creek Sagers Killetie, because "killetie" was Dutch for "small brook." Later, the Sagers Killetie was changed to Sagers Kill, than to Sage Kill, and finally to Saw Kill.

Initially locals welcomed the notoriety of Woodstock's streams as the income from visiting anglers lined their pocketbooks. Many boarded hunters and fishermen in their homes and served as their guides. Later, visitors stayed in inns and shopped at stores. While anglers could stay at the Woodstock Inn right in town, many choose an inn operated by the widow of Eli Barber located on the banks of the Esopus, just north of The Corner, or the point where Woodstock's Beaver Kill flows into the Esopus at Mt. Pleasant. At that time, the Beaver Kill was known as the Barber Bush Kill. Anglers, who stayed at Barber's, hired a horse and wagon and fished the Beaver Kill up through De Vall's Hollow to Mink and Silver Hollow.

Austin M. Francis, in his 1983 book, *Catskill Rivers: Birth Place of American Fly Fishing*, mistakenly places the Barber's Inn, on his hand-drawn map of the Esopus River, at the mouth of the Bushnellville Creek in Shandaken, labels it as the first fishermen's inn in American, and dates its opening to 1830. He also attributes its ownership to Milo Barber. Similarly, Alf Evans, Woodstock town historian for many years, wrote in his 1988 book, *Woodstock: The History of an American Town*, that anglers stayed at Milo Barber's Inn located at The Corner. Milo Barber did open a small store along the lower Stoney Clove Creek in 1826, but I didn't find a record of his license to operate an inn. Eli Barber was licensed to operate an inn at The Corners in 1810 and after he died his widow ran it for many years. Also unlikely is that Barber's Inn was America's first fishing inn. Inns in Pennsylvania, especially near the spring creeks in Carlisle (the real birthplace of American fly-fishing), catered to fishermen in the late 1700s. Sam Carman's tavern, on the East Connecticut River, subsequently renamed Carman River, also catered to fishermen in the early 1800s.

An 1874 article in the *New York Times* described Ulster County's Saw Kill and Beaver Kill as the best fishing rivers near New York. After the Rondout and Oswego Railroad laid tracks as far as Phoenicia in 1870, anglers could take the train to Mt. Pleasant and fish Woodstock's Beaver Kill upstream from The Corners. With their waters now crowded with outsiders, local Woodstock anglers were increasingly concerned about their streams.

The growing reputation of the area's excellent fishing resulted in the land owners putting no-trespassing signs on their riverfront properties. In 1875 the *Kingston Freeman* printed the proper legal form for such signs, perhaps the first source of posted signs in the country. Nevertheless, bragging by local anglers was frequently reported in the *Kingston Freeman* and contributed to the area's developing fame and to poaching on posted waters. In 1879, Woodstock fisherman Fred Happy boasted of catching close to 200 fish in a single day on the Saw Kill. In 1884 George Mead, owner of the second largest hotel in the area, bragged that a boy caught "the largest trout ever caught on top of a mountain" near his hotel. In 1894, Marshall Roosa took a 24-inch brook trout from the Saw Kill just below the village by "guddling," a method later declared illegal. The method clearly speaks to the "gullibility" of brook trout. The angler stokes the fish for prolonged periods until it can be caught with the bare hands. Roosa spent nearly half a day working for this trophy trout. I would be willing to bet, however, that Roosa's trout was a brood fish stocked either by the state or a private hatchery as Catskill streams simply didn't produce fish that size.

## Accommodations and Other Activities

Except for the angler who fancies small-stream fishing in relatively rugged environments, most visitors to the Catskills should consider fishing these streams as other activities. The native and holdover fish in all of these creeks can be difficult to catch, not because they are sophisticated, but because they feed in places difficult to cast to. Anglers who have progressed from catching lots of fish, to catching big fish, to catching selective fish, and who now want to catch difficult fish, will find the creeks challenging. The fisherman who needs overnight accommodations can select from those listed in the three chapters devoted to the major Catskill rivers.

If fishing the lower Rondout, the D&H Canal Museum is located in High Falls. The small museum features a 45-minute walking tour that includes the sites of five old locks. On display inside are canal boat models, old photos, and other historical information.

Even though the Saw Kill is now a put-and-take trout stream, the village of Woodstock is worth a visit. Woodstock lies below Overlook Mountain, first used as a hunting ground by the Algonkian-speaking Esopus Indians, who lived along the banks of the Esopus near the Hudson river, and later used for hiking and mountain climbing by numerous summer tourists. The Woodstock Tannery was the catalyst for the town's development and those early residents who did not work for it produced gun powder

from the stems of local alder trees.

Woodstock is perhaps best known for the 1969 Woodstock Festival and its 500,000 attendees. Nevertheless, Woodstock was a flourishing cultural center long before the famous rock concert. It was noted for its Indian Caves, the Overlook Mountain House, Off-Broadway theater, the Byrdcliff and Maverick Arts Colonies, The Art Student's League of New York Summer Landscape School, and as a community that attracted artists, musicians, social reformers, and assorted intellectuals.

Today Woodstock embraces traditional small town life, but with an added dose of the arts. It boasts fine gift shops, good cafés, and excellent restaurants. It also has one movie theater.

Near Woodstock is Opus 40. Harvey Fite, owner of a six-acre site that includes an abandoned rock quarry, constructed walls of a stone linked together in intricate designs. Stone-lined pathways lead up and down and around pools and the summit is dominated by a nine-ton monolith. Fite worked on his sculpture for 37 years, leaving it unfinished when he died in the early 1970s.

The view from the site of the Overlook Mountain House, which is 50 feet higher than the more famous Catskill Mountain House, is the only spot in the Catskills that provides an unbroken view of all points on the compass. The view covers the states of Vermont, Massachusetts, Connecticut, New Hampshire, New York, New Jersey, and Pennsylvania and all 100 miles of the Hudson Valley. The initial popularity of the Mountain House, completed in 1871, extended southward the mountains considered part of the Catskills.

# CHAPTER SIX

# The Mighty Delaware

## *Three Rivers in One*

By now, most anglers know that the Delaware's two upper branches, the East and West Branches, are tailwater rivers that, with sufficient releases of water from the depths of the reservoirs above them, can remain cool in the summer months and also cool the Main Branch below them. Three Delaware System Reservoirs collect water from a 1,200-square-mile area. Two of the reservoirs became operational in 1955. One was formed by a dam across the Neversink River. The other, the Pepacton Reservoir, was formed by the Downsville Dam across the Delaware's East Branch. The Cannonsville Reservoir, formed by a dam on the West Branch of the Delaware, became operational in 1967. These reservoirs feed eastward through three separate tunnels to the Rondout Reservoir where the Delaware Aqueduct begins. This 84-mile-long aqueduct conveys water south to the Kensico Reservoir in Westchester County. From this reservoir the water is chlorinated and flows further south to the Hillview Reservoir in Yonkers.

The water system also includes water from the Catskill and Croton Watershed Systems. The entire system is gravity fed, enabling tenants on the forth floor of New York City building to get water simply by turning on the tap. When the system was first built, many borough buildings were kept at four stories so that water pumps would not be needed. The system's 21 reservoirs have a total capacity of 600 billion gallons, with New York City residents, along with those living in towns along the river in Westchester and Putman County, using approximately two billion gallons of its water each day.

To fully comprehend this enormous

use of water, Kenisco Reservoir, which holds 31 billion gallons, is only a 15-day water supply. Hillview Reservoir in Yonkers, with its 900-million-gallon capacity, would be used up in 11 hours. In situations of severe drought, even if the Reservoirs were completely full at the drought's onset, they would be completely empty in 300 days and ten million people would be without water!

Fearing drought, the city used to keep the reservoirs as full as possible, but a governmental decree in 1964 required that the city release sufficient water, from the reservoir of its choice, to maintain a minimum flow in New Jersey. This flow prevents the upriver encroachment of the salt water line into a large aquifer lying under southern New Jersey and into municipal water intakes drawing directly from the river. It also allows the use of river water by downstream agriculture, industry, recreational, and power companies. The decree, however, did not state that the flow had to be continuous, and often it wasn't. Large amounts of water were often released, followed later by smaller amounts, adversely affecting

*Spring-creek conditions on the East Branch of the Delaware above Shinhople.*

both the cold and warmwater fisheries. In addition, in years of severe drought, maintaining the stipulated flow rate downstream required releases that lowered the reservoirs beyond their ability to replenish themselves and the city faced serious water shortages that they handled by releasing as little water as possible.

Under pressure from anglers, New York state passed legislation in 1976 that resulted in larger releases from the dams during some periods. Under drought conditions, however, the releases are sharply reduced to a Basic Conservation Release, a flow rate that causes thermal stress for aquatic life in the summer, as well as contributes to the formation of anchor ice in the winter.

## The East Branch

A "Me and Joe" article on the East Branch appeared in a major outdoor magazine in the early 1970s. It described fall camping on the river just below the Dam on the Papacton Reservoir and spoke of catching large rainbows at dusk. The writer thought the really big ones that were caught had washed over the dam. However, campfires are prohibited anywhere on reservoir property and the trout season ends on September 30. Special permits are required to fish the reservoirs and the riverbeds adjoining them. The area just below the dam is reservoir property. Sections of the river further downstream that flow through private property can be fished, but camping on the riverbank requires permission from the land owner. There are no rainbows in the upper East Branch or in the Papacton Reservoir and the first mile or so below the dam is the nursery area for brook and brown trout. Further downstream decent size browns can be caught, both stocked and wild, but rarely rainbows. The reservoir, itself, is famous for its large brown trout (as are many of the city's reservoirs), but these big fish are caught at night, on large saw-bellies, and few wash over the dam. My distrust of sports writers was born upon reading this article!

The East Branch fishes like a spring creek. The flow of the river is slow and with proper releases, the water is cold. But because Pepacton water is purer water than Cannonsville water, the Big Apple hoards every drop and the river can warm up substantially when high-water conditions result in water running over the top. The warmwater significantly affects the emergence of hatches and the dry-fly-fishing can become poor.

But, when the water temperature is right, the East Branch is a challenging river. Entering a long pool downstream from rising fish sends a wave upstream that spooks the wary wild browns. The task is to slowly wade within casting distance of where a fish rose last, and then, to wait patiently until it rises again. Then the angler will have one, and only one, cast in which to catch the fish before the spooking sequence starts again. And if weed growth is high, as it typically is by summer, the big fish the angler does manage to fool often breaks-off in the weeds.

At dusk, these fish move into shallow water to feed on hatching flies, water you would normally walk through to reach the pools below the riffles. Good-sized fish can be in ankle-deep water near the banks. Their ingestion of the small flies hatching in the shallows is subtle. They simply rise up, raise their heads, suck in the fly and ease back down, causing only slight, but perceivable, changes in the current flow. In shallow water, nymphs are concentrated from top to bottom in only inches of water, making them easy targets. I usually inspect such areas before I walk through them, remembering the old adage, "Fishing is not just casting." But sometimes, in my impatience to get to the good water, I fail to heed my own advice. A big brown scurries beneath my feet and I curse a lost opportunity.

While I find the long runs challenging, I end my day on the East Branch fishing a relatively deep channel (on the East Branch deep means waste deep, even in relatively high water) along an island where I can mindlessly cast a weighted nymph to the far bank and let it drift downstream. At the end of the island is a short riffle (most riffles on the East Branch are short) that fish move into from a pool below. Here the fishing is not so difficult, a few stocked browns can be caught, and I usually go home not getting skunked.

Tom, who camps on the river and fishes it more than I, has taken browns up to 17 inches. Others who have taken even bigger fish include Bill Durato, developer the Durato Hare's Ear, a fly tied with a grizzly hackled tail and wodduck wings, who died last year at the age of 86 after becoming a fixture on the river, and Frank Mele, with whom Bill shared a fishing camp on the river and who authored the book with a title close to my heart—*Small in the Eyes of a River*.

One bonus to fishing the East Branch is that a bald eagle or two can usually be spotted. Bald eagles had disappeared earlier from the Catskills and were close to extinction in New York State. During the 1980s, 200 birds, mostly from Alaska, were introduced into the state. By 1994 there were 23 active nests in New York, with several along the East Branch.

*Small brown trout hold in step pools on Eastern Catskill's Sawkill Creek.*

*A northern pike caught in April stripping a fly slowly along the bottom of Lake George's Harris Bay.*

*Bob Young working a run on Upper Rondout Creek.*

*Bob Young stalking wary Upper Rondout Creek wild trout.*

*Art Flick matching the hatch with one of his Catskill flies.*

*Schoharie Creek flowing through the most scenic region of the Catskills.*

*Wading to the tops of one's waders is often necessary to reach rising holdovers in the Beaverkill's Wagon Tracks Pool.*

*Willowemoc Creek at the Livingston Manor covered bridge.*

*Scott Daniels casting to cruising browns in the Ausable's Island Run.*

MIKE ZELIE

*Art Flick unhooking a small Schoharie brown.*

*Each fall, the short stretch below Moose River's Brassua Dam gives up a number of landlocked salmon.*

*The famous Five Arches Bridge over the Esopus.*

*The Housatonic at Dead Man's Hole.*

*Esopus pocket water below the Bend Pool.*

*A Lake Champlain landlocked salmon.*

*Sandy Bardy Royster braving a fresh snow in search of Salmon River steelhead.*

During the 1980s, great blue herons also made a comeback along the river. Unlike their smaller cousin, the green heron, they fly from the river's edge to the treetops when I get near to where they are feeding. While I enjoy the majesty of the bald eagle and the grace of the great heron, my favorite water-side bird is the hooded merganser. I just love to watch a mother bird and her young chicks, all nodding their heads in unison, swimming up and down the river, apparently going no place in particular but simply out for an afternoon swim.

### The BeDel

The section of the East Branch flowing from its junction with the Beaverkill to its junction with the West Branch at Hancock, is called The BeDel by many anglers. By late June the Beaverkill above this section is quite warm and any remaining browns have moved elsewhere, but as soon as the cool water of the East Branch joins the Beaverkill, the river teams with trout, both wild rainbows and wild and stocked browns. It is now a freestone stream with classic riffles and runs for 15 miles until it joins with the West Branch to form the Main Stem.

There is a section on the BeDel where I can park, look down a steep, vegetation-free riverbank, and spot fish rising at the head of a long pool. One evening, I arrived at this spot and a number of fish were feeding. About 75 yards downstream, the river can be entered without damaging the steep bank directly below the pull-off. From this spot, anglers can walk upstream along the river's edge or fish their way upstream to the head of the pool where most of the fish are rising.

One day, when I was readying myself to fish the run, an elderly couple

*Anglers working nymphs from a drift boat on the BeDel above Hancock.*

pulled their travel van into the parking spot, got out, and began assembling their fly rods in company with me. After I was rigged up, they asked me where I was going to fish. I replied that since they were visitors to the area I would give them first choice.

Pointing to the fish rising below, the old man said, "How about directly below where we're parked?"

I said, "Go ahead, I've fished this spot before and can do so another day. I'll enter the river from a spot above the run and fish my way upstream from there."

I left while he and his wife were still rigging up. Upon entering the river, I looked back and saw them, one at a time, repelling down the steep bank with a rope that was fastened to the side of their van. I wondered if they planned to go back up this way, and, if so, if they'd have the strength to pull themselves up using the same rope?

I hooked the only two rainbows that were rising in my section and returned to the pull-off, intending to drive to another spot. Just as I reached my car, the man's head suddenly appeared from directly below the parking spot, followed shortly by the rest of his body. He had, in fact, used the rope to pull himself up the bank. He then hollered to his wife below, hit a button, and up she came. I saw that the rope was attached to a winch that hauled his wife directly up the bank. He said that, in several years, he would need a remote to start the winch as he, like his wife, would then need this assistance.

About a mile above Hancock, there are rapids followed by a long, deep pool that is fished regularly by Lynn Tomkins, who lives about 40 minutes away in Pennsylvania. Almost any evening during the season Lynn's 1984 silver Ford 150 pickup will be parked at the lot next to this stretch. If you don't see him in the river, look for him on a bench along the bank. Lynn, a thin man, will be dressed in light brown, wearing light-brown hip boots and a brown baseball cap. He stays on the bench he brings until he sees a rise and then casts to it with a soft-hackle fly. More often than not, he hooks and lands a big trout. Anglers often tie dry flies for Lynn, but he never uses them. He settled on this stretch some years ago because he likes to catch big fish and he believes there are more big fish in this run than anywhere in the Delaware system. Lynn's devotion to this stretch must have put him in touch with its water spirit because I have never caught a fish over a foot long in it!

### The West Branch

Ever since New York City was required to release cold water from the Cannonsville Dam each year after June 15, or whenever the water temperature in the river exceeds 75°, the fishing in both the West Branch and the Main Stem has significantly improved. But there were never good ole days on the West Branch because the river below the dam was too warm before the reservoir was built to support trout. When the Cannonsville reservoir was first built, water was released for short periods when the reservoir was full, the few trout remaining in the summer would go into thermal shock, and the water would rapidly warm again. The smallmouth disappeared and by July the water upstream from Hancock contained few fish. I fished the river off-and-on during this period and usually caught a few skinny browns in the section just below the dam. The fish were like ice cubes when you handled them—it wasn't worth the four-hour round-trip.

Thanks to the efforts of fishermen to obtain stable water releases, the West Branch and the Main Stem below it are now considered the best native rainbow rivers in the East, providing the water conditions are good, meaning that the water is easily waded and the temperature has stabilized. I cast for rainbows in the riffles, the pools immediately below, and the short runs between the islands just upstream of Hancock. If I want browns, I travel northwest to the no-kill section at Deposit and fish a deep pool in a river bend. In the hour before dark, using an emerger, I will typically hook a half-dozen browns, but they fight poorly in comparison to the rainbows. Hatchery fish were stocked in the no-kill section for many years and their offspring still fight like they were stocked fish. The browns I catch well below this section fight exceptionally well, often jumping clear out of the water several times before making their downstream run.

While the West Branch has been touted as the Bighorn of the East, unlike the Bighorn, where countless browns hold in the pockets and troughs between weed beds in the long, slick runs between rapids, the West Branch runs are devoid of holding trout. While large rainbows occasionally rise and even jump in these runs, they prefer to cruise up and down the length of the run rather than hold in one spot. It is ridiculous to equate the Delaware with the Bighorn because the number of fish per mile is one-tenth that of the Bighorn, significantly fewer fish are caught by anglers, and the average size of the fish caught is 12 inches. I averaged 12, 18-inch fish a day for three days on my second trip to the Bighorn and when you float the Bighorn you pass over hundreds of visible trout in the runs. In contrast, I have worked the weedy slick water at the heads of rapids in the lower West Branch, where the bottom conditions look identical to those of the Bighorn, and I have never even spooked a trout, probably because browns are scarce in this section and rainbows prefer to spend most of their time in the pools directly below rapids or in the riffles themselves.

Anglers wanting to do well on the river should call ahead for river conditions and be prepared to go almost immediately because conditions can change rapidly. For example, for several years my angling partners and I have scheduled two nights and three days fishing on the Delaware system during the third week in May. On some of these trips, the West Branch has been too high and too cold to fish. On others, the water has been low and the water temperature in the seventies. One hot May, the stonefly hatch was so thick at night that no one could get gas

in the local station because millions were flying around the lights above the gas pumps, and crawling, and creeping on the ground below.

One weekend in early June, when it was close to 100° in Hancock, I could barely see the river through the fog. I had been told that after the cold water has been running for 48 hours, a good sulfur hatch occurs. The fish will have acclimated to the cold water and will feed voraciously. I cautiously entered the high, cold water, but the fog was so thick that I could see neither my hand in front of my face nor my feet in the water. When the fog parted a bit, no sulfurs were hatching. Shivering from the cold, even in the 98° heat of the early evening, I climbed onto the riverbank and was greeted with a nauseating blast of warm air. I forgot how hot it was outside when immersed in a giant air conditioner!

I have visited the West Branch on several midsummer days. One early evening in July, I caught two 15-inch rainbows on an emerger in a run along a small island, followed by two 14-inch rainbows on a hair-winged caddis just before dark in the fast water below. I got so turned on that I returned to the same spot the next night. Unlike the previous evening, there were no fish rising in the run. On a weighted nymph, I took two 16-inch suckers in the run and two ten-inch rainbows in the fast water. A week later at the same spot, I took six rainbows in less than an hour from the fast water on nymphs, but none were more than ten inches. That's how it is on the West Branch of the Delaware!

## The Main Stem

The Main Stem before June 15 is predictably unpredictable. In fact, it is unpredictable even after the fifteenth of June. The river is characterized by mile-long runs with riffles between them, and only several islands throughout its length. When a hatch begins, big fish move into the riffles and the slick water just above and below them. While some trout dwell in the riffles, particularly the long riffled sections above Lordsville and Kellam's Bridge, most stay in the heads and tails of the long, slow, deep pools in between. I have seen huge trout come clean out of the water in these long runs, perhaps for a dragonfly or to escape an even larger fish, or maybe just for fun, but I have never been able to catch any. By now I should know better, but it's hard to resist putting your fly where a once-in-a-lifetime fish just jumped.

The distribution of trout in the Main Stem is perplexing, even before the rainbows migrate upriver to the cooler sections in response to the summer sun's warming of the water. Only specific and relatively small sections of this large river contain browns. I have never caught a brown near Lordsville, a rustic hamlet named after Eleazor Lord who started the Erie Railroad, and I caught my first wild brown above Kellam's Bridge just this year. Tom also landed a brown this year that was close to 19 inches, seeing it rise in the tail of a pool as he was walking back to camp just before dark. At dusk, the browns tend to feed in the tails of long pools and more often than not, we are fishing at the heads of pools.

Browns are stocked in most of the tributaries to the Main Stem by both border states, but I have never taken a brown near the mouths of these tributaries. In addition, the tributaries to the Main Stem are so low in the fall that the browns typically spawn in the Main Stem. Because the river bottom can change from year to year, the Browns

may have to move large distances to locate new spawning sites. As a result, the browns end up in different locations every year.

The rainbow population begins to thin at Callicoon, but anglers do catch them as far south as Port Jervis, 40 miles downstream from Callicoon, where canoe rentals and bass fishermen flourish. I turned the biggest rainbow I have ever seen in the Delaware while streamer fishing for smallmouth in the rapids just below the mouth of the Mongaup Creek. I talked to a man who doesn't fish (they are very trustworthy), who lived next to the Mongaup. He told me his son caught rainbows more than six pounds in the Mongaup on nightcrawlers in the early spring just below the dam of the Rio Reservoir. He said this without any fanfare, as if it were an everyday occurrence. If he had been telling me this story in years past, I might have been suspicious because the Mongaup Valley was a center for hemp growing, largely to make rope, but also to make marijuana, to which many early Americans, including George Washington, were strongly addicted.

Callicoon was once a thriving river town, and while abandoned buildings adorn its banks, it has managed to reinvent itself. I would characterize the town as hard and raw. Some of Callicoon's hard residents still think they live in the old days. I was looking for coffee one morning and the only store open in town was a small bar. I asked the barmaid if she had any and she nodded affirmatively. I stopped her, as she began to pour me a cup, to ask if she had any brewed that was decaffeinated. She eyed me suspiciously and replied, "Real men don't drink decaf!"

Callicoon is named after the old Dutch word "Kollikoon," which means

MELODY MORDOCK

*A solitary angler on the Main Stem above Kellam's Bridge.*

"wild turkey," because many of these big birds were seen along the banks of the Callicoon Creek by early Dutch travelers. As a result, the Dutch first called the stream Kollikoon Kill, or Turkey Creek. Actually, the word literally means "crackling hen" and I can still hear the barmaid barking at me to drink regular coffee! On a 1779 map of the area, the creek was called—you guessed it—the Beaver Kill!

Fish average 15 inches on the Main Stem, with many of the larger rainbows caught before sunup by live bait fisherman. In the late 1970s, before strict limits were placed on keeping Main Stem trout in 1995, I arrived at the river one spring morning and two bait fishermen were leaving the river with a string of rainbows, all over 20 inches. It almost made a bait-slinger out of me.

Jim Merritt, a contributing editor to *Field and Stream*, reports that his best day on the Main Stem was a 23-fish day on a float trip. Nevertheless, his Main Stem catch rate is about one trout for every three hours of effort, a rate somewhat better than the one trout every five hours revealed by angler surveys. Merritt's biggest West Branch trout to date on a dry fly is 15 inches and his best Main Stem trout is 18 inches.

I have hooked rainbows over 18 inches in the Main Stem on only one occasion. On this occasion, I was fishing the tail of a run about 50 yards above Little Equinunk Creek, a small creek that joins the river from Pennsylvania just above a rapids. The rapids continue for about 100 yards followed by a very long, deep pool under Kellam's Bridge, one of those pools where enormous fish occasionally jump once, but you never see them jump again. I had taken one of two 14-inch rainbows that were rising in the run and had followed the fish downstream through the first part of the rapids. Fourteen-inch fish give you quite a battle in the Delaware's fast waters.

After netting the rainbow, I looked downstream and saw Tom frantically waving to me from his position in the pool just below the bridge. I could not hear what he was saying, but after he stopped waving, he cast, and I saw his rod bend with a big fish. I now knew he was beckoning me to join him. I stumbled along the rocks, walking downstream as swiftly as I could, watching him play and land his fish, cast again, and immediately hook another.

As I crossed the Little Equinunk, I saw what was happening. Thousands of spent flies were floating down this small feeder creek and disappearing into the rapids. I surmised that the fish in the pool were gorging on those flies that survived their cruise downstream. Upon reaching the upper section of the pool, I was treated to a symphony by slurping trout. One after another, they sucked flies from the surface of the ruffled water.

I waded in and cast a small, brown spinner to the biggest slurp I heard. An immense rainbow sucked it in and took off downstream where it jumped and tore the hook loose. The second noisy slurper I hooked did the same, only this time the fly broke off. The third and fourth fish straightened the small hook. I did manage to land several smaller fish before the noisy river quieted and the last spent spinner floated by.

I waded down to where Tom had just landed his last fish. He just shook his head. In a 90-minute period, he lost the biggest rainbow he had ever seen and he netted, as well as lost, a number of good sized ones. He even hooked two American shad that, surprisingly, sucked down his small spinner imitation. This annoyed him greatly because the first shad took so long to land that he missed many opportunities to cast to large trout. When the second shad hit, he deliberately broke it off.

Several years ago, our group rented two drift boats from a fly shop near Hancock and floated the Main Stem. Mike and Scott drifted the river from Hancock to Buckingham and we drifted from the Buckingham Access to Long Eddy. It was very hot and the low water was unusually warm. Tom caught an 18-inch chub and Bob got bored and caught shad in the riffles. But our float was not a failure, because we could show Bob the ancient and tat-

tered inn where Tom and I liked to stop for a burger in Long Eddy, an archaic, largely abandoned, river town. The inn looks like it's about to slide down the street into the river and the bar inside it is a long wooded one with a tin roof painted to look like copper. A large photo of the town, taken when it was a bustling center of activity in the 1800s, hangs on the wall. It's like stepping back in time.

On this visit to the inn, I didn't enjoy my lunch because a deputy sheriff sitting next to me at the bar talked loudly on his cell phone throughout our entire meal. He was trying to convince his boss that he needed backup to remove an encroacher from an old trailer. Evidently, the unwanted squatter was a local with a mean temper who felt entitled to stay in trailers seasonably occupied by others. The deputy was worried that he would get shot. No new information was communicated after the first minute, but the deputy droned on and on to delay the inevitable.

Very few flies hatch during the day on the Main Stem so most anglers toss nymphs into the runs at the head of pools. I like to sit and watch Mike Zelie fish such spots. I appreciate the disciplined manner in which he tosses his weighted nymph upstream, guides it back through the current while intensely watching his line, picks up the line at the end of its float, and casts it again. It is mesmerizing to watch the repetitiveness of this sequence of activities. I know that if the fish are feeding where Mike is casting, he will hook one. When he does, I rig up and join him.

On a fall trip in 2000, I had my best evening on the river, hooking three rainbows just under 18 inches on a green Woolly Bugger and landing two of them. Earlier in the day, we had fished in the run below the mouth of Basket Brook. In the flat water above the creek's mouth, we saw large rainbows cruising in the flat water. We didn't even bother casting to them, knowing that such efforts were fruitless.

## Shad on the Fly

During the month of May, anglers can catch fish between three and five pounds, but the fish won't be trout, they will be shad. American shad migrate up the Delaware and can be hooked on a wet fly almost anywhere above Port Jervis. When I first fished for them, I concentrated on the BeDel in a section behind a rest stop on Route 17, just below the hamlet of East Branch, a section called Cemetery Pool by locals because of the few grave stones passed on the walk to the river from old Route 17. The section is popular among Livingston Manor and Roscoe fishermen because the migrating fish can be easily seen in the early evenings as they move up the far bank of this long, slow pool. The shad fly can be cast to visible fish, the pool can hold many anglers, and the fish can be fought in the calm backwaters, enabling others to continue fishing.

"Here comes a small school," hollers the angler closest to the tail of the pool, and everyone gets ready for action. Readiness largely means peering down into the water with polarized sun glasses and then dapping the shad fly in front of the unsuspecting fish. Most of the fish pass unscathed through the gauntlet of anglers.

Examination of the stomachs of shad verify the view that shad do not feed during their migration and that they are exclusively plankton eaters while in the ocean. It remains a mystery why one shad in a school will

suddenly suck in a swinging fly while others ignore it. Some postulate that the fly is grabbed out of annoyance. But, as mentioned earlier, Tom hooked two on a small spent spinner. I can't believe that shad would be annoyed by a spent spinner on a pool's ruffled surface. Those that inhale the angler's fly, if hooked, make several long runs downstream. I say if hooked because shad have soft mouths and the hook easily tears loose if set too hard.

While shad remain in the pools during the day, often swimming up and down in them, they cannot be caught when engaged in this seemingly aimless, circular activity. The best time to catch them is when they move upriver from pool to pool in the mornings and evenings. Polaroid glasses are essential and there can be no wind. If the water surface is rippled, the small schools of shad cannot be seen as they pass by. If the wind doesn't die down in the late afternoon, a trip to the river has been wasted.

One weekday evening, in the late 1970s, I had the Cemetery Pool all to myself. Two trout fishermen wandered down from the fast water above, watched me for a while, and then said, "May we ask what you are you doing? We see you casting a short line, almost dapping it, in the middle of this long run, and we can't figure out what your trying to accomplish."

"I am fishing for shad," I replied.

They were from Connecticut, their names were Allen and Jeff Passante, and they were fishing for trout. They had never fished for shad. This was surprising because shad fishing originated on Connecticut rivers. The Salmon and the Connecticut rivers, followed by the Scantic, Eightmile, and East rivers were the Nutmeg State's traditionally good rivers for shad. I showed them how to rig up, gave them a few shad flies, and got out my camera. At first, neither Allen nor Jeff could see the shad, but once I pointed out their gray shapes (they look bluish-gray from above but they are actually silver), they spotted them easily. I have seen anglers in the Beaverkill working for trout completely unaware that shad are all around them.

After Allen and Jeff each caught two shad, we were joined by George Wells, owner of a local hardware store, who took his normal place at the tail of the pool. George always arrived earlier than other local anglers, making sure he got the spot where he would be the first to see the shad as they entered the pool from the riffle below. I preferred being further upriver because it gave me more time to get ready, but George felt that the fish struck more upon first entering a pool. He landed two while I took his picture. After the photo session, I fished alongside George and my two pupils, but I didn't hook a single shad that evening or on my next visit.

Sixteen years later, Jeff published an article in *Fly Fisherman* describing fishing on Connecticut's Housatonic, and two years after that, a guide to fishing the river. I mention both works when I discuss the 'Hous in Chapter Eight, but I didn't realize, until I looked at my labeled slides in preparation for this chapter, that he was one in the same.

Just before my Uncle Jim's death, I took him to fly-fish for shad at the Cemetery Pool. Jim taught me to fly-fish when I visited him in California as a boy, but he had never fished in the East nor had he fished for shad. Some might interject that, when knowing the former, the later can remain unsaid because shad are native only to the Atlantic ocean. Nevertheless, in 1871,

eight cans of newly-hatched Hudson River fry were transported to California by an enterprising character named Seth Green, and introduced into the Sacramento River. Now they are distributed from San Diego to southern Alaska. California anglers can cast for them in the American, Russian, and Feather rivers, but my uncle, who lived outside of San Francisco all his life, had never done so.

Because Jim was in his nineties, he experienced difficulty wading out through the shallow but wide pool to get within casting, actually dapping, range of the channel along the far bank. It was an easy wade for the rest of us, but he slowly waded along, both going out and coming in, taking my arm without complaint as he did so. Had I anticipated his struggles, I might have taken him elsewhere. We caught no shad, nor did anyone else in the pool. Most of the time a gusting wind made it impossible to see below the surface.

I apologized for subjecting him to such drudgery. Two long hours driving up, difficult wading, two hours of waiting for fish, and two hours of driving back in the dark. He admonished me for my words, repeating that he had a good time. He enjoyed seeing the famed Catskill rivers and the Delaware Valley on the way up. He said he hadn't had such good exercise in a long time because he now fished from drift boats. He enjoyed the stiff breeze in his face, and, most of all, enjoyed my enthusiasm for his favorite activity. He then reminded me that fishing wasn't all about catching fish!

I haven't been to the Cemetery pool since I took Uncle Jim, wanting to leave the pool to his memories. Since then, I have learned how to catch shad during the day, leaving the evenings hours free to cast to rising trout. There

*George Wells proudly displaying a typical BeDel shad.*

are several bridges that cross the Main Stem where one can look down and see the shad holding behind a particular rock. If fishing with a friend, one of us will stay on the bridge and spot for the other the schools below. If I go first, I cast the fly downstream so that it swings behind the rock where the shad are holding. My lookout above on the bridge guides each of my casts. The trick is to swing the fly right past the shads' noses. If the school is spooked and moves to another rock, my lookout tells me to move with them. We take turns until all the schools have moved from under the bridge or until the trout start rising. I have also learned to find shad holding at the heads of shallow riffles. Once found, I repeatedly dance a weighted shad fly in their faces until

one hits, a mindless activity that can be done when trout fishing is slow.

## Accommodations and Other Activities

There are several state campgrounds near the Pepacton Reservoir, a reservoir named after John Rice Burroughs' novel, *Pepacton*, the story of a rafting expedition down the East Branch. Two are the Miller Hollow Campground (607-363-7492) and the East Branch Campground (607-363-7561). Five private campgrounds are located along the East Branch above and below Al's Wild Trout Limited, a full-service fly shop in Shinhopple. Al Carpenter writes a weekly e-mail report (alstrout @catskill.net) and has an web page (www.catskill.net/alstrout).

*A lone shad fisherman on a BeDel pool.*

Two campgrounds above Al's are within walking distance of the lairs of some of the river's largest browns, the Delaware Valley Campground (607-363-2306) and the Catskill Mountain Kampground (607-363-2599). Both are about three miles south of Downsville, with the CMK being the larger of the two with 1,500 feet on the river. Just below Al's is the Peaceful Valley Campsite (607-363-2211), (www.peaceful-valley.com) the biggest on the river. Its property includes three river islands and its amenities include a swimming pool, playgrounds, canoe rentals, adjoining hiking trails, and a Blue Grass festival in July. Terry's Shinhopple Campground (607-363-2536) is located just below it and the Oxbow Campground (607-363-7141) is located two miles below Terry's.

The Downsville Motel (607-363-7575) is owned by Al of Al's Wild Trout Limited and a small tackle shop is attached to it. Melanie Carpenter actually runs the motel, rents its canoes, and sells its tackle while Al is down-stream at his larger shop in Shinhopple. The Old School House Inn and Restaurant, within walking distance of the motel, serves a variety of beers. Pepacton Cabins (607-363-2094) (www.catskill.net/pepecton) are located on the river two-and-one-half miles north of Shinhopple on River Road. Those wanting to stay at the juncture of the East Branch and Beaverkill can choose the East Branch Motel & Log Cabin Tavern (607-363-2959). Jerry's Three River campground is located in Pond Eddy (607-557-6078) on the BeDel.

Before you travel to the West Branch, call its hotline number to obtain information on water releases (607-467-5565). There are several motels and fishing lodges in Hancock. The motels include the Capra Inn Motel (607-637-1600) on Main Street, Smith's Colonial Motel (607-637-2989) two miles south of the bridge over the East Branch on State Route 97S, and the Timberline Motel (607-467-2042) near Hales Eddy. From the last two motels, you can walk to the river. From Smith's you enter the main branch below the Bard Parker Pool.

Lodges include The West Branch Angler and Sportsman Resort, a resort for the whole family near Deposit that includes three miles of private access on the New York side of the West Branch, a complete fly shop, a heated swimming pool, boat rentals, and hiking and biking trails. Al Caucci's Delaware River Club (800-6-MAYFLY), just across the river from Hancock, includes a fly-fishing school affiliated with its fly shop. Scott and I once camped at Caucci's and we each caught two nice browns in the evening right off our site. The Starlight Lodge (717-798-2350), also across the river from Hancock, offers excellent dining.

In Deposit, the angler can choose from three inns, all on Oquaga Lake. The largest is Scott's Oquaga Lake House (607-467-3094), a full service resort on 1,100 acres. The Chestnut Inn (607-467-2500) is a small inn and Alexander's Inn (607-467-6023) is a four-room bed and breakfast.

The upper Delaware angler and his family will find limited after-dark activities. The towns of Hancock and Deposit both have no significant evening activities except dinner, cocktails, and bed. Hancock has a nice Italian restaurant on a hill just north of the Hancock Exit on Route 17, an excellent family restaurant in the village, and at least one decent bar and grill. Deposit has only a Wendy's and an ice cream parlor.

The one place to stay in the village of Callicoon, the Western Hotel (845-887-9871), has only six rooms and reservations must be made in advance. The hotel was built in 1825 and has been nicely restored. Near it is the 1906 Restaurant that opened in 1998 in an historic building on Main Street. Joe McFadden's Fly and Tackle Shop (845-887-6000) is on the river at Hankins, just above Callicoon.

Those who want to keep family members occupied can stay at the Villa Roma Resort and Conference Center (845-887-4880) or the Hills Callicoon Center (845-482-9985), both near Callicoon. The Villa Roma has indoor/outdoor pools and tennis courts, a golf course, a health club, children's programs, nightly entertainment, and a disco club. The Hills Center is much smaller, but still has a pool, tennis courts, and nightly entertainment. They can also stay in one of 21 log-cabin-style rooms at the relatively inexpensive Eldred Preserve (800-557-FISH). Its property contains two bass lakes, with the lakes listed on the 25-best-places-to-fish list, three stream-fed ponds stocked with trout, and a small section of a trout stream. Boats to fish on the lakes can be rented for $60 for an eight-hour day or included in the room rate with a package deal. The Eldred Preserve is located southeast of Callicoon, off Route 55, eight miles south of Route 17B. Camping anglers can stay at the Upper Delaware Campgrounds (845-887-5344) in Callicoon on the river's edge.

Outside of hotel functions there is little to do at Callicoon. Anglers can take their families to Callicoon Center, northeast of Callicoon, and visit the Apple Pond Farming Center (845-482-4764) where crops are grown organically and animals roam freely. Wagon rides can be taken around the property and border collies can be watched herding sheep. There is also a petting farm and a native American gift shop specializing in sheep-skin products. Arrangements can be made in advance to stay overnight in their guest house.

# CHAPTER SEVEN

# The Esopus
## *A Miniature Steelhead Fishery*

Back in the 1970s, I loved both the Esopus and the drive to it, particularly when I drove up and over the Shawangunks, where the Slide Mountain massif is viewed on the descent into Rondout Valley. Slide Mountain, the largest mountain in the Catskills and the source of the Esopus, drains 50% of the Catskills. The mountain got its name following a landslide in 1820 that carried away a large portion of the mountain's northwest slope. From the Rondout Valley I took one of several different roads until I reached Samsonville Road, an intriguing road that runs beneath the east slope of High Point, a mountain containing a spring that ebbs and flows with the tides, winds through Goblin Gulch, and ends up at the southwest shores of the Ashokan Reservoir into which the Esopus Creek runs. Others must have loved the river too as 60% of anglers who fished it

during opening week for its magnificent spawning rainbows were not from the immediate or surrounding area.

I joined Trout Unlimited because of this suburb river. Catskill Chapter members, such as Art Flick, Bob Dyer, and Jud Weisburg, were stewards for the river prior to my membership, as was Michael Migel, editor of *The Master's on the Dry Fly* and *The Stream Conservation Handbook* and founding director of the American League of Anglers. Mike was a frequent guest of Art Flick at his home on the West Kill and he accompanied Art to the Trout Unlimited chapter meetings in Kingston. Upon his return to New York City, Mike would report the status of Esopus issues to the membership of the Theodore Gordon Fly Fishers, as they, too, loved the river and always took part in battles to save it from threatening hazards.

## The Portal

In 1924, The City of New York completed an underground aqueduct between Schoharie Reservoir and the Esopus Creek. The outlet is known at the "Portal" and it releases water from the Schoharie Reservoir into the Esopus about 12 miles about the Ashokan Reservoir at the hamlet of Allaben. The aqueduct, a horseshoe-shaped, concrete-lined tunnel, more than eleven feet high and ten feet wide, was blasted through solid rock for most of its 18-mile length. The aqueduct's deepest point is 2,200-plus feet below the summit of the 3,200-foot mountain located just east of Deep Hollow Notch near the hamlet of Westkill. If the sticks of dynamite used to blast the tunnel were laid end to end, they would stretch for 525 miles and if the cement used to create the tunnel's 10-inch-thick walls were loaded into freight cars, the train would be 25 miles long.

Up until 1976, a keeper, whose living quarters were built above the 175-foot-deep intake shaft, operated the gatehouse over the inlet to the aqueduct on the Schoharie Reservoir. Eight brass gates were located in the shaft, through which the water passed into the aqueduct. When water was called for, the keeper would take water temperature and turbidity readings, turn the values, and open one or more of the gates. The roar of the water being released far below would shake the windows in the apartment.

When all the gates are wide open, 650 million gallons of water pass through the Portal each day, about a third of the amount used in one day by consumers of reservoir water. Prior to the 1990s, when the portal was wide open, the river became turbid and the fishing difficult. The Schoharie river itself drains a region of clay soil. Harry Albert Haring, in his 1931 book, *Our Catskill Mountains*, wrote that he always knew when the portal was open because the Esopus water was gray. Arthur Nue, wrote, in *Field & Stream* in 1938, about his experiences on the Esopus, "before they carried the water from the Schoharie Reservoir miles through a tunnel and dumped it into the Esopus, which until then was one of the finest trout rivers I ever hope to see." Nevertheless, the general opinion was that the river benefited from the cold water. During the summer months, when releases of at least 200 million gallons were needed to keep the water cool, many anglers were attracted to the river.

During the 1990s, massive flood damage created serious bank erosion along several streams that flow into the Schoharie Reservoir and releases from the Portal have made the river murky for much of the season. The very condition that created the river's wonderful

*Angler nymphing for wild rainbows holding in the shaded pool beneath the famed Five Arches Bridge.*

fly-fishing now adversely affects it. Fortunately, a number of stream reclamation projects are underway on the feeder streams to the Schoharie and the flows from the Portal should become clearer in the near future.

The Esopus also runs gray for several miles below the village of Phoenicia after rain storms wash clay from the banks along Warner Creek, a tributary to the Stoney Clove-Chichester Creek, that flows into the Esopus at Phoenicia, but they gray water is an occasional event, easily compensated for by moving up or downstream. A storm restoration project on the Warner Creek, scheduled for 2003, might clear up this longstanding problem.

Recent state surveys show no decline in the number of fish caught in the Esopus, or in their size compared to past years, but they do reveal that fewer fishermen visit the river. I fish the river less, not just because the water is often murky, but because I believe that fewer big rainbows visit the river during late spring and early summer. During major river hatches, rainbows from the reservoir would enter the river to feed, with most confining their activities to waters below Cold Brook. In addition, young Esopus rainbows used to stay in the river until they were about ten inches and then migrate downstream to the Ashokan Reservoir, in contrast to steelhead smolts that swim to the sea when they reach two inches.

Most of the juvenile trout feed on tiny crustaceans (zoo plankton) and transparent water fleas (daphnia) that flow through the portal from the Schoharie Reservoir. As they grow bigger, they begin to feed on flies. With increased siltation the fly hatches have decreased and I believe that the juve-

nile trout leave the river earlier in response. The birds that feed on the river's hatches also have changed. In the 1970s, numerous barn swallows, with their deeply forked tails, used to dart to-and-fro over the waters, attracted to the river from their nests on nearby buildings by the heavy insect hatches. Now they have been replaced by the cliff swallow, a square-tailed bird that lives by the river and has few food choices other than swarming insects.

I talked to a salmon-egg fisherman near the Trestle Hole in early November of 2000 who had caught 20 rainbows, all between seven and eight inches. He planned to return later in the month when he thought bigger fish might be in the river. Using a Hair's Ear and a Glow Bug, I hooked only two rainbows in the turbid water on the same day. In the 1970s and 1980s, bait fishermen usually out-fished me when flies weren't hatching. Now they out-fish me all the time.

In years past, the 12-mile section below the portal, called the Big Esopus, was the home for 100,000 wild rainbows. But, anglers caught only about 7% of them. Consequently, the state stocked, and continues to stock, 28,000 browns in the spring. Most of these are caught within several weeks of stocking and those not caught perished shortly thereafter. Because of the stocked trout's vulnerability to both angler and river, holdover browns represented only 3% of the catch.

Some anglers might scoff at ten-inch wild fish and claim that nothing of value has been lost, but ten-inch wild Esopus rainbows, particularly those caught well below the portal, are solid silver and fight like miniature steelhead. In addition, when the water is clear, it is a splendid river. In spite of development along its banks, its many

*Early spring pocket water at Elmer's Rapids just below Phoenicia.*

rapids, long stretches of pocket-water, long riffles, rocky banks, and deep runs flow through many forested sections, providing shaded bank cover throughout most of the day.

## The Challenge of Catching Migrating Wild Rainbows

In late winter and early spring, rainbows leave the Ashokan Reservoir and return to the river to spawn. Few of the big spawning fish are caught. Between the mouth of the Esopus and the famous Five Arches Bridge in Boiceville, a distance of eight-tenths of a mile, approximately 500 heavily-clad souls each fished for two hours and 15 minutes during one April and came up with about 75 rainbows, only ten of which were more than 12 inches, and no wild browns. This amounts to one-tenth of a fish per fishing hour. But, an estimated 7,000 wild fish were in this section during that April! When artificial-lure-only regulations were introduced in the same section, the catch rate per hour dropped to one-twentieth

of a fish, even with the addition of 1,000 stocked browns. Arnold Gingrich, confessing his failure to capture Esopus rainbows, remarked in *The Well-Tempered Angler*:

There were many other places, on the Esopus and its tributaries, where the trout would school up by the hundreds, lying motionless in the current, but nothing I could throw at them would attract their attention.

Because of its discerning wild rainbows, the Esopus offers a challenge unparalleled in Catskill Mountain streams. Theodore Gordon, writing in *The Complete Fly Fisherman: The Notes and Lectures of Theodore Gordon*, predicted in 1913 that:

By the way, the new Shokan dam, in the Catskills, will afford the finest trout fishing in America, if properly treated and not spoiled by the introduction of other predatory fish. It will be stocked naturally from the

Esopus with the rainbow and European trout of good size and quality.

Since the time of Gordon's prediction, Esopus Creek's wild trout have been mentioned in more than two dozen books. Ray Ovington devoted a full chapter to the river in his book *The Trout and the Fly*. In Cecil Heacox's *The Complete Brown Trout*, we learn that in 1918 the dry-fly rod was developed while fishing the Esopus and that the Fanwing Coachman was designed in Phoenicia. Preston Jennings, who laid the foundation for American angling entomology with his *A Book of Trout Flies*, published in 1935, lived in Woodstock for a while and his studies included the waters of the Esopus. Ernest Schwiebert's *Matching the Hatch*, which first appeared in 1955, was inspired by Jennings' work. This work, along with *Nymphs*, Caucci and Nastasi's *Hatches*, and Swisher and Richards' *Selective Trout*, incorporated studies of Esopus insect life.

While the "hogs" are tough to hook, enough spawner fish are caught to maintain the angler's interest. A fellow Trout Unlimited member, Tom Emerick, fooled a 23-inch, four-and-one-half-pound female on a size-8 Hare's Ear in Broadstreet Hollow Brook, somewhere below Nannette Falls, named for an Indian women who sold trinkets to tourists in the late 1900s.

Anglers working the Esopus in April when the water is high will experience difficulty both wading and keeping the fly on the bottom. The Esopus is subject to great rise and fall, with flooding capable of causing considerable streamside damage, even floating away bridges. In the Blizzard of 1993, almost two feet of snow fell in March on Slide Mountain and a county snow plow was buried under eight feet of snow on a local road above the river. In sharp contrast, when it rains less than an inch in April and the Portal is closed, the Esopus can be so clear and low that stoneflies dance on the water's surface and fish can be caught on a Sofa Pillow.

Whenever I arrive at the Esopus on an early spring day, it seems inhospitable, but when I notice the wild onions and purple violets pushing their way out from under fallen logs, the green mosses growing along the edge of the creek, and the footprints of small animals along the sandy shoreline, I begin to feel I belong. My feet get used to the ground's undulations as I walk along the bank, stepping over fallen branches and around large clumps of river-flushed debris, and when I wade into the river, I feel that my life has begun again.

### The "Hogs"

Emerick's 23-inch fish was a big rainbow by fly-fishing standards, but the real hogs that used to travel up the Esopus from the Ashokan were rarely caught. Ashokan is an Iroquois name that means "place to fish," but even anglers trolling saw-bellies, the abundant baitfish upon which the rainbows now feast, rarely hooked them in the reservoir's upper basin. I don't know the size of the biggest rainbow ever caught in the watershed, but a former state-record brown came from the river's famed Chimney Hole, located just above the river's mouth. It was just two ounces shy of 20 pounds.

Rainbows from the Ashokan's lower basin, school-up each spring at the Dividing Weir in an effort to reach the upper basin so they can enter the Esopus to spawn. Some of the rainbows gathered there in the 1970s and 1980s

SCOTT DANIELS

*Durae Daniels, Montana Fish, Wildlife and Parks staff member, fishing the Esopus on a break from studying the habits of Flathead River bull trout.*

could consume Emerick's fish. Anglers lined the shoreline below the weir and ploped lures and live shiners into the midst of these frustrated fish. Although I watched this annual event for a number of years, I never saw any of the really big ones caught.

Rainbows, having relatively small mouths, no longer grow as big in the reservoir as they did twenty years ago. Alewives, that have replaced golden and emerald shiners as the preeminent bait fish in the reservoir, grow to large sizes rapidly, preventing the rainbows from gorging themselves on them as they did on the smaller shiners. But they are still big by normal standards. On opening day of 2000, I witnessed two anglers fishing from a boat in the lower basin just below the weir. The two anglers boated 22 pounds of trout in less than an hour. The biggest was six pounds. I also spoke with a mealworm fisherman from New Jersey who caught a 25-inch rainbow at the creeks mouth that same spring.

Over the years, my longtime companions and I have caught several respectable rainbows in early spring, with the biggest being a 19-inch fish taken by Tom Royster on a stonefly nymph cast upstream in the riffle below the Trestle Bridge. Tom also caught a large walleye on the very next cast.

The Black and White, Esopus, and Phoenicia Bucktails are well-known streamer patterns that were developed on the Esopus. They were designed in the 1930s before state biologists discovered that the Esopus contains few minnows. I believe that dace, darters, fallfish, juvenile suckers, and other small fish cannot adjust to the constantly changing water flows in the Esopus and that the turbid water prevents the growth of nutrients needed by them to grow.

Before I knew this fact I often stopped at Folkherts Brothers, a landmark general store in Phoenicia, to buy streamers. Dick and Herman Folkherts owned the store for many years. The brothers always had a good supply of flies tied by two local anglers—Ray Smith and Ralph Hoffman. Ray liked to boast that his red face was not the result of his fishing in the sun, but the result of his mother love's for his father, who was half-Cherokee. His grandfather was a full-blooded Cherokee. Ray tied close to 12,000 flies a year and developed his own version of the Red Fox.

## May and June

During early May, the countryside evolves from its bleak gray to a roof of green, all shades of it, from yellow to blue, that block the view of the reservoir and the mountain homes above it. Tulips, forsythia, dogwoods, and lilacs appear in succession and accent the unfolding green. Eventually, the pale greens in the mountains turn into deep Kelly greens, and full spring arrives.

Although the river still experiences hatches of traditional mayflies, they are meager and sporadic. The best hatches are now the flies of the *Isonychia* family. The *Isonychia bicolor*, imitated by the Slate Drake or by Art Flick's Dun Variant, hatches in June. Nymph imitations work best, even when the hatch is in progress.

After buying a sandwich at the Boiceville Market, I eat it as I walk a well-worn trail along the river to see if fish are rising. The quarter-mile stretch contains a long, deep pool, pocket water, and several rapids. Rainbows feed along the entire length of its far bank, one of the few places where rainbows can be hooked in slick water. I introduced Walt Joseph, a professional colleague of mine, and Scott Daniels to fly-fishing in this stretch and they both caught a foot-long trout in the pocketwater. Scott switched to a salmon egg and caught an even bigger one.

Scott was a skilled warmwater fisherman when we first met, but he liked to fish for trout on opening day, casting salted minnows under the bushy banks of a county stream. Upon learning that I was a trout fishermen, he asked me to join him on a stream that ran through private land. When we arrived at the secret spot, there were more guys along the little stream's bank than I have ever seen on opening day. The owner must have given permission to the whole county. I left the congregated pack and headed upstream to seek some privacy. I came upon an old refrigerator that had tumbled down the bank into the stream. Inside its open door was a brook trout. I had caught trout living in culverts, but I could not bring myself to cast to one living in an ice box. I told Scott that next year he could accompany me!

On rare occasions, I would hook a streamborn brown that, until I see its magnificent coloration, I think is a rainbow because it jumps and races downstream. For the last several years, the state has been stocking 15-inch browns below Cold Brook, but they are poor substitutes for these magnificent wild fish. I vividly remember each wild brown I have fooled in the Esopus because I have hooked so few. The best fighter, a fat 15-inch fish, I caught on a Black Gnat, a fly I haven't used since. Ray Bergman writes that we don't use black-colored flies as often as we should and I am no exception to his conclusion. But on that day, I was casting the gnat upstream while struggling against a fast current that ran along the boulder-lined bank northwest of Cold Brook. I was searching the high water with a fly I could see while looking into a gray glare. All of a sudden I could no longer see the gnat, I raised my rod tip and immediately was into this strong

*A wide-open Portal in July draws anglers to the river during the hot summer months.*

fish. A strong fish in the strong Esopus current is exciting and thinking about it still gives me a thrill!

### July and August

Every river has its river-lore and the Esopus is no exception. There are stories of expert fishermen who catch big rainbows in the summer. My favorite is the one told some years ago about an angler who, each July, traveled from New Jersey to the Esopus, rented a trailer at the Sleepy Hollow Campsite, and caught a dozen rainbows over 20 inches in the nearby waters. Don't believe such stories. Creel census studies by the New York State Department of Environmental Conservation estimated a zero catch for rainbows over 12 inches during the summer months and electrofishing during the same season turned up very few trout over a

foot long in any of the sections studied, data clearly refuting the tale of the visiting expert. Most big trout, whether browns or rainbows, prefer the Ashokan Reservoir to the river, even in the days when the water was clearer and the hatches prolific.

During early July, I occasionally hook a fish over 12 inches from the fast pocket water and Melody hooked an 11-incher while carrying her chaise-lounge over to a gravel bar with her rod tucked under her arm and her line dragging behind her. Fishermen watching loudly complained that it wasn't fair. I have seen bait fisherman catch rainbows over ten inches on a worm fished on a three-way swivel above a heavy weight and dropped into very turbulent water. At dawn, on July 2, 1982, Roger Lapp, of Cottekill, New York, landed an eight-pound, 15-ounce

Those rainbows that remain in the river dwell in the fastest water. They will not rise to the borrowing nymphs hatching along the banks and eagerly taken by the stocked browns. A rainbow will dart out from a hiding place to strike only at a fluttering caddis, and if the fly drags before the rainbow grabs it, the rainbow will be seen no more, no matter how good the next several floats. In contrast, a stocked brown will make a number of passes at the same fly, drifting motionless in the water along the banks, until it is hooked in its ignorance.

The Portal brings refreshingly cool water to the Esopus in the summer and, while I don't catch many fish, I enjoy wading in the river's rushing currents. Lee Wulff, who fished the Esopus in the 1930s, said that he "loved to get in the water and wade upstream for the sheer exercise and joy of wading." I also enjoy watching the ungainly heron, gingerly tip-toeing on the flats, in search of prey, and the wood ducks and other water fowl floating downstream to feed in different spots.

*A mysterious pool on the "Little Esopus."*

rainbow that measured 27 inches. Lapp hooked it on a nightcrawler in the section below the Five Arches Bridge. Its estimated age was six years, one year over the life expectancy of Esopus rainbows. So there are some large ones in the river during the summer, but not a dozen 20-inchers to be taken by one visiting angler in one small stretch of water. Several good spots to pick up larger rainbows are the channeled rapids below the mouth of the Woodland Creek, those above and below the Five Arches Bridge, particularly those near the Bend Hole, and those above and below the Chimney Hole.

## Fall Run Rainbows and Browns

The Esopus is one of the few rivers where large browns can be caught in the fall. Although the angling season closes September 30 on the feeder creeks, it stays open until the end of November on the Esopus. Many of the browns stocked in the reservoir remain in it throughout their life, especially those stocked in the lower basin, but some stocked and wild browns from the upper basin do migrate up the river to spawn in the fall. Those who fish near the mouth of the river have the best chance them. In the fall of 2000 I spoke to several anglers who reported catching browns over 20 inches at the river's mouth. One angler, using roe removed from the first female he caught on a salmon egg sac, landed several that size.

Anglers also catch big rainbows in the fall, as a small but significant number accompanies the browns on their spawning run. Fall-caught rainbows were believed to be those that fed on the roe of brown trout, but I never believed this theory. Why would trout that could get fat feeding on saw-bellies in the reservoir bother to swim up a river to ingest a few small fish eggs? A clue to another theory is that fall-caught male rainbows show the lower jaw extension and hooked-nose characteristics of spawning fish. In the late 1970s, my conversations with fisheries biologists outside of the local region revealed that a small percentage of rainbows partially ready for spawning migrate up tributaries from lakes and reservoirs in the late fall and remain in the rivers over the winter. The large majority die, but the ragged survivors ensure the species continuance should some catastrophe prevent the spring run of their siblings. There is now increasing evidence that Esopus rainbows, rainbows that spring from the same prehistoric sea-going ancestors as Pacific Coast Steelhead, actually run the river between September and February and spawn from late winter to early spring.

*Isonychia harperi* hatch from late August through early October, particularly on overcast and drizzly days. While this fly crawls out of the water onto a rock to transform into a dun, a slate-bodied Compara-dun will fool fish when breezes blow the naturals back into the river. The angler who becomes weary casting a Leadwing Coachman or a Zug Bug can switch to a floating pattern, such as Art Flick's Dun Variant, and be almost as successful.

Fishing in the fall on Eastern rivers presents a special challenge. Hundreds of leaves, accompanied by seed fluffs that early settlers collected for their medicinal value, drift on the breezes, with many alighting on the water and floating downstream. My fly floats only for a moment before it catches a leaf. Leaves waffle through the air behind me when I hook them on my back-cast. At times, I am startled by strong winds that blow branches from trees and by squirrels that drop acorns from them. When the leaves become so thick that a free-float becomes impossible, I stop fishing and enjoy the flickering pattern of the dancing leaves as they float down from above and feel glad to be alive.

## The Esopus in the Old Days

As I emphasized in earlier chapters, before the early 1900s, very few people fished today's famed Catskill rivers. There were no real roads and few places to stay. Even if there had been, the sun-up to sun-down work ethic restricted leisure time activities. The few roads that were eventually built by the tanning industry were too rough to be traveled by horse-drawn carriages. In fact, the roads were so poor that the hemlocks, cut down for their bark, could not be transported out of the forest for use as lumber. Close to 95% of them just lay where they were cut to rot.

The Esopus Kill, its original name, was no exception. Before the tanneries, the Esopus above Kingston flowed through forests heavily timbered with hemlock and interlaced with trees that had fallen naturally along its banks. Because of the canopy, created by the large oaks and maples in the lower sections and the huge hemlocks in the upper sections, spring melts were more gradual and the creek less swollen. Consequently, the creek bed was small, with numerous ledges that created waterfalls and step-pools, and contained large boulders. In fact, the word Esopus comes from a combination of Native American words that mean "small river."

It must have been a truly exquisite stream, but one with few big trout. Many of the streamborn flies captured by Preston Jennings in the 1930s would not thrive in such pristine waters nor would baitfish have the necessary foods to grow large. It undoubtedly was an excellent brook trout stream, but the tanneries, the lumber mills, and one man, R. L. Livingston, changed all that!

The area's first tannery started in Shandaken, followed by the Phoenix Tannery in 1836 in Phoenicia, the namesake of the town, and by several others. Not only did the tanneries pollute the river, but numerous saw mills were built along its banks. Because it was expensive to move the lumber to the mills, the mills moved to where the lumber was cut. Mills were hastily built, wood was cut, and when the wood supply was too far upstream from the mill to be easily moved to it, a new mill was built upstream and the old mill abandoned. As a result, the riverbed was cluttered with both abandoned and working mills, as well as with sawdust and slab wood from the mills themselves.

## Changing the Riverbed

Robert L. Livingston, through his wife,

Margaret Maria, (who was the daughter of the man who swore in George Washington as president and later became Chancellor of New York City), owned 66,000 acres in Woodstock and adjoining Shandaken and Olive, including Slide Mountain. In an effort to profit from his land, Livingston planned to make use of the cut hemlocks that lay wasting in the mountains. Hemlocks were used as hexagonal paving boards on Broadway, creating a possible market for his lumber. But first, he needed to find a way to transport the logs to Kingston, where major lumber mills were located and where lumber was shipped to New York City. In 1833 he started the Esopus Creek Navigation Company whose first task was to widen the Esopus, eliminate water falls and step pools, and remove boulders and other hazards that would interfere with raftsmen guiding lumber down the creek.

Between the end of August and the beginning of November of 1837, the company blasted a channel from 30 to 50 feet wide on 23 miles of the river, but Livingston never lived to see his dream realized. A minor economic depression left him cash-strapped. The few logs that Livingston did manage to move to the river were moved at a ruinous expense and his company folded. King Solomon said that "Where the tree falls, it lies. It is done, and we will not rise it up again."

## The Railroad and
## the Boarding Houses

Austin Francis, in *Catskill Rivers: Birth Place of American Fly Fishing*, writes that in the mid-1800s, anglers took a steamship from New York City and then a stagecoach to Phoenicia to fish the Esopus. This statement is misleading. Although the river was no longer

*Nymphing the Esopus downstream in the channeled section at Mt. Tremper.*

cluttered with saw mills or wood waste, Livingston's channeling had seen to that, it was still polluted from tannery waste and most of its native brook trout had died. In fact, when Kingston residents had need for additional water in the 1883, Esopus water was too polluted to use so the Saw Kill was damned and a reservoir created in nearby Zena. In addition, only the very wealthy could afford a trip that took the better part of two days. But even after 1870, when railroads shortened the travel time, anglers did not fish the Esopus. They lacked both the vision and the equipment to do so, but primarily, they lacked the interest.

Most visitors to the Catskills were fresh-air seekers first, sight seekers second, and outdoor enthusiasts third. They came primarily to escape New York City's summer heat, not to fish. Many found that a stay in the Catskills could improve their physical health. Consequently, lodges played up their cool locations. Those along the Stoney Clove Creek, for example, advertised their distance from a narrow section of

the creek that remained frozen over in July and August. Anglers hiked into the small creeks where cool air greeted them, walked along their banks, dapping their bait or flies into the most convenient spots, and caught pan-sized brook trout that they took back to their boarding house to be cooked for their evening meal. Family members fished together, and ate a picnic lunch packed by the inn keeper's wife on Sundays when the mills were shut down and the water wasn't the color of chocolate milk.

Anglers used long wooden pools, mostly made of ash or lance-wood, with interchangeable tips for bait and fly-fishing. Braided silk lines and gut leaders were fitted with size 8 to 10 hooks and once a trout was caught on a fly or a worm, its eyes and fins, the fins to imitate a minnow and the eye to imitate a fish egg, were used for bait. Few anglers wore rubber boats because rubber in those days became sticky in the sun and stiff when cold. Consequently, when boarding houses advertised that their locations were on famous trout streams, they were referring to the small feeder creeks that entered the Esopus.

The majority of boarding houses, where anglers stayed for less than $8 a week were concentrated in four locations. The southern-most location was at the junction of Woodstock's Beaver Kill and the Esopus, referred to as The Corner, currently named Mt. Pleasant. The next location north was at Phoenicia, a major center for bluestone quarrying, with most of the boarding houses located north of the village along the Stoney Clove Creek. The next concentration was upriver in Shandaken Center, near the Bushnellsville Creek. Shandaken was a Native American name signifying "rapid waters" and the creek in those days fit that description. From boarding homes in the hamlet, anglers took a short buggy ride to Fox Hollow, Peck Hollow, and Broadstreet Hollow Creeks. Lament's Hotel, situated on the Bushnellsville Creek in Deep Hollow Notch (called the Smith Bush Kill at that time), claimed they were located at the "headwaters of one of the finest trout streams in the United States."

The last concentration was at Pine Hill, through which the Birch Creek flows before it enters the Esopus. Pine Hill had been less damaged by clear cutting and its inns catered to fishermen. One advertised that "nearby brooks were filled with trout" and another that it was located "between two trout streams."

Legend has it that the hamlet of Big Indian, located just below Pine Hill, got its name from Winnisook, a Native American of enormous stature. His life and death spawned three different versions of a legend. The first is that he single-handedly terrorized the local whites for so long that a major effort to kill him resulted in his death at the mouth of Birch Creek. As an example to other Indians, his assailants held him up against a large tree and crudely cut his profile on the tree's trunk. His outline remained there until the tree died and was cut up into shingles. Ever since, the area has been called Big Indian.

The second version claims that Winnisook was the first local Native American to switch from scalping to crop raising and thereby gained the respect of the white farmer. In spite of his seven-foot height and enormous strength, he was killed by wolves and buried by his brethren not far from the railway station, where a "Big Indian" was carved in a nearby tree to serve as his monument.

The third version claims that a local girl named Gertrude wanted to marry Winnisook. Unfortunately, her father had promised her to another man whom she reluctantly married. Eventually, she ran off with Winnisook and lived with him for seven years. One day her husband was searching for cattle raiders, spotted Winnisook, and shot him in a jealous rage. Wounded, Winnisook hid in a big hollow tree where he soon died. Other versions say that the husband hid the dead body in the hollow tree. Gertrude discovered his body in the tree, had him buried nearby, and she and her children lived near the pine tree for the rest of their days.

H. R. Winter, a physician and skillful upper Neversink angler, wrote an article on trout fishing that was partially reproduced in the widely read 1879 edition of Van Loan's *Catskill Mountain Guide*. He wrote that two friends vacationed for six weeks in Phoenicia, fished two days a week, from three to five hours each day, and caught nearly

2,000 brook trout. Although fishing writers exaggerate, lots of brook trout were caught in those days, particularly when the state stocked thousands of brook trout in nearby creeks, more than 30,000 in some creeks, and the lodges paid private hatcheries to supplement their stockings. Dr. Winter's piece stimulated many Catskill visitors to try their hand at trout fishing. The introductory section of the piece reveals the difference between anglers who fished the Catskills and those who fished the rugged Adirondacks.

Parties coming to the mountains seeking rest of mind, improvement of health, and desirous of pleasure and amusement will find that trout fishing is one of the best and most profitable recreations in the country, Those who have tried it universally admit that there is no recreation which will relieve the mind of care and anxiety equal to it.

Only a few anglers fished the Esopus for the small numbers of California trout, as rainbows were called in those days, that were first stocked in the Catskills after 1875. In some years, as few as 500 rainbows were stocked in a ten mile section of the river, while brook trout were stocked in the feeder creeks by the thousands. Many of these anglers were visiting Frenchmen and the descendants of those who followed their benefactor, Augustus A. Guigou, to America. Guigou hired French immigrants to work in the tannery he started in Pine Hill and later in his large hotel. These Frenchman continued to use the old 15-foot wooden rods, dappled bait over the newly stocked rainbows, and later the stocked browns, who were no smarter than the wild book trout, and

took their catch back to the boarding houses that catered to them. Frenchmen were still fishing that way when I first fished the Esopus, although the rainbows were now wild fish and fewer fell prey to their technique.

Many of the valley's creeks, local land marks, towns, streams, and even mountains were named after residents, both permanent and nonpermanent, but nothing seems to have been named after Shandaken Valley's first resident, Conrad Meisner. Conrad came to the valley, did his thing, and left no mark that can be identified. That's the way it is with most of us.

## Getting There and Getting Started

To reach the river, exit the New York State Thruway at Kingston and follow Route 28 north for about 16 miles to the hamlet of Boiceville, named after an early settler. To fish the river near the Five Arches Bridge in Boiceville, turn left at 28A (the first flashing light) which leads to West Shokan. Shortly after crossing over the defunct Penn Central railroad tracks just past the river, is a place to park.

If you have a permit to fish New York City's reservoirs, you can fish downstream from this spot. With no permit, you can fish upstream. Instead of parking, turn right on Cold Brook Road and drive up the road that parallels the southwest side of the river until it ends at the Cold Brook Bridge. Cold Brook is not a brook but a former railroad station. It was a large shipping point for quarry stones from nearby mountains. You also can access the river by this bridge off Route 28 just above Boiceville. Both Route 28 and Old Route 28 (Route 40) parallel the river along with the railroad bed.

Consequently, the 17-mile section of the river from the Ashokan Reservoir to Big Indian can be entered from many spots without crossing private land. The river above Big Indian is posted.

Application blanks to obtain a reservoir permit can be picked up by turning left at Reservoir Road at Winchell's Corners (the flashing light in the hamlet of Shokan), crossing over the Dividing Weir on the reservoir, bearing left, and taking a road downhill to the Ashokan Reservoir Gate Chamber Building of the New York City Department of Water, Gas, and Electricity. The angler must then mail the completed application to a Kingston address and the permit will be mailed back.

## Accommodations and Other Significant Activities

Motels, with from seven to 14 rooms near the river include the Reservoir Motel (845-657-2002) in Shokan, the Trail Motel (845-657-2552) in Boiceville, the Cobblestone (845-688-7871) on the Chichester Creek, the Phoenicia Motor Village (845-688-7772), the Appletree Inn and Efficiencies (914-688-7130) in Shandaken, and the Starlight Motel in Big Indian (845-254-4449). You can also stay in one of the second floor rooms in the Phoenicia Hotel (845-688-7500), that still look like they did when last refurbished in 1936, or The Manor House Bed and Breakfast in Chester (875-688-2085). Further upriver, The Val D' Isere Inn and Restaurant Francais (845-254-4646) with four rooms, and the nearby Ramble Brook House (845-688-5784) with three rooms, provide intimate lodging, as does the Mountain Brook Inn (845-688-5100). Inns in Pine Hill include

the Pine Hill Arms Hotel (845-254-4012) and the Colonial Inn (845-254-5577).

Those who plan early can stay on the Big Esopus at the Lazy Meadows Cottages (845-688-9950), Mt. Tremper Pine Cottages (845-688-3678), or Ray's Cabins (845-688-5410). The Silver Creek Cottages (845-688-9912) are on the Chichester Creek and the Weyside Cabins and Motel (845-254-5484), off County Road 47, parallel the upper Esopus between Shandakan and Big Indian. The Weyside has large efficiency cabins on the shores of a small pond next to the Esopus. At Big Indian are the cabins operated by Cold Spring Lodge (845-254-5711).

Those wanting more than a place to sleep can make reservations at the Cooperhood Inn and Spa (845-688-2460) in Allaben and stay in country elegance at its finest. It has a pedestrian swing-bridge over the Esopus to a private island, a heated 20-yard indoor pool, a sauna, Jacuzzi, and tennis court, and it is open year-round. Nearby is Margo's Hungarian/German Restaurant and Sports Bar.

To provide a spouse with a real treat, I recommend staying at the Onteora Mountain House. The Onteora Mountain House (845-657-6231), located on Piney Point Road in Boiceville and built in 1929, has a bluestone foundation, bluestone and tree trunk pillars, and cedar shake shingles. It provides a panoramic view of five mountain peaks and each of its five rooms is named after each of the peaks. *Travel + Leisure* rates it in the nation's top ten.

Campers can choose from one of two state campgrounds. The Woodland Valley Campground (845-688-7647) is located at the end of the road that parallels the creek. There are several trailheads at the campground. At the

Kenneth L. Wilson State Campground (845-619-7020), located off Wittenburg Road at Mt. Tremper, family members can boat, swim, or fish in a lake and young children can enjoy a children's playground. Private campgrounds include Circle Pete's Recreation Park (845-688-5000) in Phoenicia and, if a trailer is desired, the Sleepy Hollow Campsite (845-688-5421) below Phoenicia.

On the way back from picking up a reservoir application or watching rainbows at the Dividing Weir, anglers might treat their wives to a stop at Winchell's Corners where three stores are located. The first, Winchells Corner's, sells collectibles and antiques, as well as ice cream and sandwiches. The second, the Ashokan Artisans next to Winchell's, sells fine crafts. The third, Moose Crossing, across the street, sells antiques and furniture.

The Giant Ledge Trail that starts about seven miles up County Route 47, the road that goes along the upper Esopus above Big Indian, provides a nice view of Woodland Valley and the creek below. Hikers can park just below a hairpin turn in the road. The trail is short, about a mile and a half, but it is steep. Those wanting a longer hike, with views of both the Esopus and the Village of Phoenicia, can assess Panther Mountain trail at the same location. It is a six-mile round-trip and takes about four hours. Further up the road is Slide Mountain Loop that goes to the mountain top and provides spectacular views. Native Americans called the Catskills the Land in the Sky and the view from Slide Mountain summit makes the reason for their name graphically clear. One can see all 98 Catskill's peaks, the Ashokan Reservoir, the Hudson Valley, the Hudson Highlands,

Mt. Everett in Massachusetts, and the Berkshire, Green, Shawangunk, and Taconic mountains, and on exceptionally clear days, as far as New Hampshire. Completing the seven-mile hike takes close to six hours. When finished in the evening, hikers can dine at one of three nearby restaurants, two of which are associated with inns—the Alpine Inn Restaurant, the Forsthaus Restaurant at the Slide Mountain House, featuring German cuisine, or the Mountain Gate, featuring Indian food.

Those family members who would rather float the river than fish it, can rent tubes from the Town Tinker (845-688-5553) in Phoenicia. Anglers who want to completely avoid the tubers can fish the river above Allaben or near Boiceville, where, unlike the narrower Battenkill, tubers don't really bother fishermen.

For a brief period in the 1980s, a good friend of the river and long-time member of Trout Unlimited, Jerry Bartlett, operated the Esopus Flyfisher on Main Street in Phoenicia. After he closed the shop, he continued to guide on the river, to run the Two Brothers Fly Fishing School, and to look after the river's welfare. Jerry died prematurely of a heart attack a short time after I last fished with him behind the Boiceville Market.

His widow, supported by Trout Unlimited members and others, established a memorial fly-fishing library in his name at the Phoenicia Public Library on Main Street. Tom Emerick, who had his rainbow mounted, donated it to the library where it hangs today. The Catskill Fly Fishing Center and Museum, located on the Willowemoc Creek, also has a display case at the library.

# CHAPTER EIGHT

# The Housatonic
## *The Creation of a Trout Fishery*

Marginal waters can be made into trout waters when large trout are stocked. Connecticut's Housatonic River is a testimony to this fact. The section of the Housatonic that was a natural trout stream in the old days, the section that inspired Charles Ives to compose a symphony, is miles up the road in Massachusetts, and to find trout in this section one would have to travel back in time to before the large paper companies discharged untreated acid waste from their mills into the river and poisoned it for many miles downstream. No, it is not the cooler upper sections that have made the river famous among Eastern fly-fishermen, but rather the section miles downstream in Connecticut's unspoiled Housatonic Valley. Normally a river this far from its source is a warmwater fishery, and the blue-ribbon waters of the Housatonic would be just that if left to Mother Nature.

When I first fished the river in the early 1970s, the state of Connecticut stocked 24,000 brown trout above Cornwall Bridge. Most were between seven and nine inches, but some were larger. Earlier stockings of tiger trout failed and stockings of fingerling trout only resulted in anglers catching larger smallmouth! A Bitterroot strain of brown trout, raised to withstand high water temperatures, were eventually stocked. The river was a put-and-take fishery and by the fall all the trout had either been caught, washed downstream by high water releases, or succumbed to the summer's heat.

Before the Connecticut Department of Environmental Protection first created what is now called the Trout Management Area, or TMA, tissue studies of stocked trout caught in the valley revealed toxin levels unfit for human consumption. These toxins were traced to a General Electric plant upstream in Massachusetts. The paper mills perished, but another polluting industry took their place. In light of these findings, the state stopped stocking the river in 1980 and the trout disappeared. Pressure from anglers, most notably the Housatonic Fly Fishermen's Association, resulted in restocking and designating the TMA, about a ten-mile section, as catch-and-release fishing. The lower three-and-one-half miles of the TMA were designated fly-fishing-only in 1981.

For years most trout did not survive the summer heat. Connecticut Power and Light and Northeast Utilities held back water from the river above its small hydroelectric dam at Falls Village and then released it when power was needed by customers. Large releases of warm water from the dam washed the cool water from the tributary mouths where the stocked trout gathered to reduce thermal stress. And, in periods of drought, the flow from the few small feeder creeks was nil. The river in the 1980s would have been better for the trout if it had been a put-and-take river, but the state did not want to sanction the eating of tainted trout. I stopped fishing the river completely for about 12 years.

Pressure from fishermen resulted in the power company stopping large water releases when the water temperature in Falls Church rose above 75°. This change occurred in the summer of 1995. Since then, fishing has been excellent on the river, and many large holdover trout are now caught, even in 2000 after the serious summer drought in 1999. With further pressure on the power company, it agreed to let the river run free in 2002.

The Housatonic was recently featured in a fly-fishing magazine under the title, "The Housatonic: The East's Best Brown Trout Stream?" The answer depends upon angler preference. I prefer the Ausable, Beaverkill, and Willowemoc because they contain wild fish. I catch mostly stockies in these Catskill rivers so I celebrate when I catch a wild one. The Battenkill, until recently, was my favorite brown trout stream. But unlike Catskill streams, where many of the browns migrate downstream, stocked trout tend to stay put in the Housatonic. The state currently stocks trout from 9 to 15 inches and some brood fish. They also stock big fish in the fall. Consequently, experienced anglers catch more and bigger fish than they do in other Eastern rivers. For example, one evening in May of 2003, I watched four anglers in the deeper water across the river from me catch six fat fish ranging from 15 to 20 inches, while I caught a dozen smaller ones.

Unfortunately, most Housatonic browns don't fight that well, particularly after being caught many times. Holdovers taken early in the season, however, can put up an adequate struggle, as can those who survive until the fall, easily differentiated from fall stockies by their more natural color. I once lost an unusually strong fish in the Corner Hole that took my line to my backing. I was using a large weighted stonefly during a *Baetis* hatch while anglers nearby were catching small browns on Tiny Blue Olives. Steve Fuchs, manager of the Housatonic Meadow's Flyshop, told me there was a 30-inch fish in the hole. Of course, I didn't believe him until last fall when I saw a huge wake moving upstream and smaller fish darting away that were feeding along its upstream course.

*Short-line nymphing below the picnic benches at Housatonic Meadows State Park.*

When the huge fish arrived at the pool I was fishing in, it went under and ignored the large streamers I threw into the pool.

Browns can spawn in the small creeks, but when the fry enter the river, they are eaten by the smallmouth and now by the bigger stocked trout. I have taken only a few streamborn trout over the years that have survived the predatory smallmouth, the summer heat, and the constant change in water levels.

You can instantly tell when you have one by the way they fight.

## Spring and Summer: Small Flies for Big Fish

The article on the Housatonic by Jeff Passante, my shad fishing student mentioned in Chapter Six, appeared in the July 1996 of *Fly Fisherman*. Jeff discussed river flows and went into depth about the hatches during each of the seasons. Jeff also published the

*Housatonic Fly Fishing Guide* in 1998. He referred to the 'Hous, as it is affectionately called, as a "rich tailwater river" and likened it to a spring creek. Nevertheless, the water held back by the dam at Falls Church never raises the section of the river behind the dam to more than eight feet in depth and when the water is released it flows downstream, like a lengthy bubble of water whose tail end passes a stationary angler some five hours after its front end. As a result, the river warms up early in the year.

To me, the 'Hous looks exactly like what it actually is—a smallmouth river that holds stocked trout when summers and winters are mild and rain fall is normal. While it can be crystal clear during the fall when rain is scarce, it is usually discolored, its rocks mossy and its currents cluttered. Cleated boots and a staff are necessary to comfortably wade it. By the fall, some sections do have eel grass that provides cover for the smaller trout, but other than the grass a spring creek it is not.

Passante was definitely on target, however, when he said to use small flies. The browns feed on the river's abundant hatches of small mayflies and a small fly is needed to match them. James Dicky once wrote, "A small fly inside the trout's mouth is better than a big one outside it." When the trout are sipping in June and early July, as they usually are in the river, I catch more trout on a size 18 or 20 emerger, usually in light green, than on any other pattern. Once in a while, particularly in the evening, the trout make splashy rises and a caddisfly will fool them, but after the major hatches in the early spring, the fish feed on tiny May flies. They also feed on midges, a fly that hatches in all types of water rather than just in cool trout streams.

In the spring and early summer, morning fishing is substantially better than evening fishing. The river cools down at night and flies hatch in the mornings. The morning release warms the river up and, therefore, hatches in the evening are light. Yet, most anglers like to fish it in the hour just before dark. In late August, the White Fly Hatch, for which the river is famous, comes in the evening, and in the fall heavy caddis hatches occur at dusk, undoubtedly contributing to the river's evening reputation.

Sometimes I fish before the hatch with flies tied to imitate the caddis larvae in its casing. Non anglers have also marveled at the works of this fly. The poet Pattiann Rogers wrote:

At the break of Spring
Caddisfly larvae, living in clear-
    water
Streams, construct tiny protective
    cases
Around themselves with bits of
    bark,
Grasses and pieces of pink gravel
    in mosaics

During May, June and early July, I arrive at the river about nine o'clock in the morning, especially enjoying the last stretch of my journey, the scenic drive from Sharon to Cornwall Bridge.

Toward the end of this drive, the road starts a deep decent from the mountain top into the Housatonic Valley. When I start down this incline, I sometimes think about Gideon Mauwehu, the leader of the Scatacook tribe of Native Americans who first moved to this valley with his people. Native Americans did not occupy the Housatonic Valley prior to the European Invasion. When colonists took over lands, the disinherited Native Americans became wanderers, often banding together to form new tribes. Mauwehu had ascended a mountain near Kent, much like the one I ascend on my way to the river, to hunt. Looking down on the valley, he realized that it was unoccupied. He went home, gathered up his family and followers, and moved to the region, inviting other Native American groups as far away as the Hudson Valley to join him. The small band's relative isolation was short-lived however, as European settlers crowded into the valley a decade later. Most of the native Americans reluctantly stayed, realizing there was nowhere else to go, and they attended Indian schools established to convert them to Christianity, and with it the loss of their unique culture.

Once I descend from the hills, I head for one of my favorite spots on the river. When there is no surface activity, I fish a caddis along the shady bank or head to some fast water and work a nymph. Almost any all-purpose pattern in size 14 will do. Like anywhere else, presentation is important. I have experienced the "other side of the river phenomenon" on the 'Hous just as I have on other rivers. My worst experience with this phenomenon was at the head of Cellar Hole. I arrived on the west side of the hole in the morning and found an angler on the east side into a good fish. I moved into position on the west side and after he landed the fish, I cast up into the tail of the rapids above the hole. When the line floated down into the head of the pool, I, too, was into a fish, but it jumped—it was a smallmouth. Meanwhile, the cross-river angler, having netted and released his fish, cast again and was immediately into another trout, a much bigger one than the first.

This experience was repeated two more times. He caught four trout in four casts while I only caught one smallmouth! And we were both using the same nymph—a Leadwing Coachman. On his fifth cast, the line straightened out at the end of its drift and I hollered out "Well, that's the end of your string." But before he could lift his line from the water, a trout struck— five browns in five casts, and who knows how many he caught before I arrived! I left to fish another spot and he was sensitive enough not to volunteer that information.

The middle section of the Cellar Hole is wide and deep when the water is high. The fish hold on the far bank, just out of casting range, rising to flies that drift into the calm water along the bank. Wading out as deep as I dare, I still cannot reach them with a good drift. One day I was fishing at the head of the hole and an angler appeared downstream from me. He rigged up and then entered a float tube. He floated out to within casting range of the feeding fish, anchored the tube, and proceeded to hook the fish I could never reach. I own a float tube, but it never occurred to me to use it for this purpose!

If I have no luck in one of my favorite spots, I head to the Sand Hole where small mayflies rise all the time, at least until the released water arrives shortly after noon, after which the hatches immediately cease, and when the hatch stops, I stop. Before leaving, I sometimes walk upstream to an island where the geese like to nest. Geese are everywhere on the river, with the males honking and swimming downstream while the females sit quietly on their nests in the bushes along the bank, barely visible, but their white tufts contrast against the brown bushes and give their hiding places away. When I think I have spotted each nest, I get a sandwich and a salad at Baird's General Store, the only local market in Cornwall Bridge, and eat my lunch at Housatonic Meadows State Park. There are picnic tables located along the river and I am usually joined by a cool breeze. Because of the constant water releases, the river is usually discolored in the spring, but it is tree-lined throughout its course through the valley and a pleasure to sit by and listen to its rumblings. For smallmouth water, it is a primitive setting, and a good place to daydream about days gone by.

On the mountain directly behind Baird's General Store are the ruins of an abandoned pioneer settlement, formerly called Dudley Town after its founders. The bygone town has been referred to as a ghost town, but all the ghosts have left to haunt are the stone foundations hidden among the forest growth. Legend has it that the Dudleys immigrated from England to America to escape a curse. Apparently, the Duke of Northumberland, a Dudley, was beheaded by King Henry VIII for cheating on his wife, the King's sister. In reality, the Dudleys who started Dudley Town were distant cousins of the cursed Dudleys—I doubt if the King even knew they existed.

The town endured for many years, but after a series of misfortunes, the surviving residents moved away. One man was killed when he fell from his rooftop. A woman died of lead poisoning. The first wife of Horace Greeley, who was vacationing in the town, was struck by lightning as she sat on the front porch of a guest house. And the wife of a New York City doctor went mad. While legend has it that the remaining residents left because they considered the town cursed, they actually left because of the poor farming conditions on top of the mountain.

When I'm done with lunch and daydreaming, I leave for home. After the water has been up for about two hours, a park worker told me that a *Baetis* hatch comes off, but the times I have stayed to verify this information, the hatch never came. In the fall, however, there is an excellent *Baetis* hatch during the day.

## The Fall Season

To take advantage of an excellent fall *Baetis* hatch, the Housatonic Fly Fisherman's Association has worked out an arrangement with Northeast Utilities to provide low water conditions until early afternoon during weekdays. If the water is high and cannot be held back, the Sand Hole, the Corner Hole, and the long run below it, and the section at the north end of the Housatonic Meadows Campground (by Monument Rock) are good spots to fish with Blue-Winged Olives

Thick caddis hatches come off in the evening, but I usually hook more fish in the late morning on *Isonychia* patterns, with a Zug Bug trailer, and in the early afternoons on Blue-Winged Olives. Caddisflies may start to rise during the *Baetis* hatch and some fish will skyrocket to this fly while their companions continue to sip the *Baetis*. In this situation, I fish with two dry flies, making it easier to see my Blue-Winged Olive as it floats next to the larger caddis pattern. After the water level reaches its maximum height, at around two o'clock (releases are later in the day in the fall), I take an hour break and then return to using *Isonychia* patterns. When the caddis hatch begins around 5:30, I usually catch several risers on gray caddis patterns, but when the hatch gets thick just before dark, the fish stop rising and feed beneath the surface.

I have my own theory about the good fall fishing on the Housatonic. Because the water warms up so quickly in the spring, I believe that flies wait until the cool water of the fall to hatch. For example, the Beaverkill is usually under 50° on the first of May. In contrast, the Housatonic can be over 60°. On true trout streams, I encounter few hatches during the fall. In contrast, on a good fall day on the Housatonic, flies can be hatching all day long, with the heaviest hatches occurring between early afternoon and evening.

The trout in the TMA are all stocked fish whose survival rate depends so much on river conditions that one-time events are frequent. I was fishing the Sand Hole one evening and my companion, Bob Young, moved into the fast water above the hole to cast into the pocket water. I was about to yell up to him that I had never caught a trout in that area when he hooked his first fish. He took five fish over 17 inches in that spot in a relatively short period. Many times, after his success, I fished the exact spot where he caught these fish, but I never even saw a trout.

I once hooked a hog behind a large boulder, but lost it when it ran under the boulder, broke off, and left the hook embedded in the rock. Because I pulled and pulled but could not move the rock, I imagined the fish to be a monster. For a while, I cast behind this boulder on every trip to the river, but I never turned a fish and eventually gave up trying. There are other spots, however, where there are always fish, unless there has been a serious fish kill. A lot of these spots are those where the stocked fish are first put into the river. The state used to stock rainbows in the river. Tom caught a bunch of them one year at Dead Man's Hole, but he never did so again. They must have just been stocked. I have never caught a rainbow in the TMA, but I saw one angler catch several just above the Church Pool, the beginning of the TMA. I'm sure they were those stocked below Cornwall Bridge by the Rainbow Club, a private organization, whose members stock rainbows up to five pounds, that had moved upstream into the TMA. Rainbows manage to survive the high water temperatures in rivers such as Yellowstone Park's Gibbon and Firehole rivers, but few survive in the Housatonic, perhaps because they are more easily caught than browns and die after repeated catching.

## The Drought of 1999

In late March of 2000, I met the only fishermen I saw on the 'Hous that day, two elderly gentlemen who were sipping tea to warm up while packing to drive home. They told me that they traveled up from eastern Connecticut this time every year and again in late November. They fished deep with large weighted Woolly Buggers on full sinking lines along the east bank in the park. They had each landed and released five fish over two and one-half pounds in the 50° water. I was not surprised because at this same time in 1999, I landed three 18-inch holdover trout in the Sand Hole, but I doubt if any weighed more than two pounds. This year all I caught in the unusually high water was a cold.

"How long were the fish?" I asked.

"Oh, we never measure the smallmouth we catch," replied one.

"Smallmouth," I said, "Didn't you catch any trout?"

"We weren't fishing for them," was

*The Housatonic at Dead Man's Hole.*

the reply. "We come here this time every year to catch big smallmouth. It's the only time we've found that you can catch them. Later in the year only small ones are found."

Now, these guys had to be exceptional fishermen, not only to catch smallmouth when they are half-asleep in cold waters, but also to keep large trout off their flies. I regret not having talked to them at greater length. If they knew how to keep large trout off their flies perhaps they also knew how to get them on! But not wanting to further interrupt their late-morning tea, a seemingly important component of their annual pilgrimage, I went on my way.

Because neither I nor the two smallmouth anglers had hooked a trout, I thought the severe drought of 1999 must have killed all the fish. I learned later that many survived, including some big ones, perhaps schooling up below spring seepage

because the feeder brooks emptied only trickles of water into the river. Howard McMillan, proprietor of the Housatonic River Outfitters, the other full-service fly shop on the river, reported that unusually high numbers of large browns were caught, particularly by drift boat fishermen casting to the banks. Mike Zelie and I both hooked trout in the fall of 2000 that were over 20 inches. Mike caught his on a yellow stonefly and I fooled mine on a size 22 all-green fly, one I sometimes use during a *Baetis* hatch when I fail to get hits to Blue-Winged Olives. I spotted an uncommonly large trout sipping *Baetis* flies in the riffles at the top of the Sand Hole. I cast to the fish a number of times and got one refusal. I switched to the solid green fly and cast again, but to no avail. I then cast to a dimple rise past the big fish and was instantly into a huge fish. I don't know if it was the same fish, but I certainly didn't care when it bolted downstream, reversed direction, and then dashed downstream again, rolling once on the surface and causing such a splash that my heart stopped.

When I finally worked the fish up to where I could look down upon it in the water, its back was so broad that my first thought was that I had hooked a carp on a dry fly. I hooked this heavy trout using a one and 1/2-ounce, full-flex rod, and quickly learned that it lacked the backbone to bring this fish to the surface to net or to drag onto the shoreline. When I moved the trout into very shallow water, it was too large to fit in my net. When I tried to plane the fish onto the complete net, a net 22 inches in length, the fish was too big to fit on it, and, in the effort, I broke the 6X tippet.

I fish the 'Hous because it is a pleasant hour's drive from my home and it can be fished year-round. When the winters are mild, as they were in 2002, the browns often feed on small midges, best imitated by a Brooks Sprout Midge or a Pheasant Tail Parachute. If the browns are not rising, I drive several more miles and ski Mohawk Mountain in nearby Cornwall. As I get older, I enjoy fishing big rivers and the 'Hous is a big river. I don't worry about my backcast or bemoan the time wasted retrieving flies from trees and bushes. When I'm up for less strenuous fishing, I head for the 'Hous. It has some great hatches, particularly in the fall, and as I continue to age, I will undoubtedly appreciate it even more.

### Getting There and Getting Started

While Great Britain has one Cornwall, Connecticut has six, but only two, Cornwall Bridge and West Cornwall, are of concern to anglers, although some anglers might like to stay in one of the two small bed and breakfasts inns in Cornwall. The hamlets of Cornwall Bridge and West Cornwall are easily reached by driving west from Torrington, east from Sharon, south from Canaan, or north from Danbury. When planning a trip to the river, anglers can call Northeast Utilities on their toll-free number (888-417-4837) and find out river flow conditions and the water temperature at Falls Village. If the water is flowing near 600 cubic feet per second, (one unit of release), wading will be easy. If flowing near 1,200 (two units of release), wading will be difficult, but certain areas are accessible. If flowing at 1,800 (three units of release), wading will be downright dangerous.

Many anglers access the TMA at the Housatonic Meadows State Park, in Cornell Bridge, with the Corner Hole in the park being the most popular spot. Others stop at the various pull-offs along Route 7, which parallels the river between Cornwall Bridge, the beginning of the TMA, and West Cornwall. In fact, the first hole upstream from the state park is called One-Car-Hole, because only one car can park in the pull-off, and the second hole upstream is called—you guessed it—Two-Car Hole. In the early spring, some anglers access the river from Beers Hill Road on the east side and either walk along the bank or use the railroad tracks to get some distance upstream.

Anglers, particularly those who like to hike, can access the river just below West Cornwall by taking a trail that goes along the river's east bank, paralleling the railroad tracks south to Cornwall Bridge. The trail is accessed by crossing over the covered bridge at West Cornwall, taking the first right (sign says "dead-end"), driving through the property of a convention center, and parking where the road dead ends. When the river is crowded on weekends, I walk this trail and usually find a secluded spot to fish. There are excellent midge hatches in the pools in this section during the winter.

Anglers wanting to fish upstream from West Cornwall can drive through the covered bridge and the hamlet, take River Road north (the turn is just before the railroad tracks), and park in the pull-offs along the river. I rarely fish this section because the water release from Falls Church arrives here much sooner than it does five miles downstream. This is the section to fish in the evenings, after the high water has passed it by and new water has yet to be released.

The river below the no-kill section can be accessed by walking along the railroad tracks on the east side of the river or taking River Road along the west bank until it becomes a gravel road, parking where the road ends, and walking east through the fields until the river is reached. Anglers sometimes hook huge rainbows in this section. Their initial surprise is followed by disappointment as the huge fish fight poorly for their size. They are hatchery-raised rainbows stocked by the Rainbow Club. Downstream from the end of River Road the water has more smallmouth than trout, but locals tell me that each riffle between Cornwall Bridge and Millford contains trout, particularly the section below the falls at Bulls Bridge, designated in 2003 as the second TMA on the river.

The Housatonic is one of the best smallmouth streams in the Northeast. With a trout streamer and a light fly rod, close to fifty bass between ten and twelve inches can be caught in the TMA on many August days. With a four-inch streamer and a long rod, less bass will be caught, but it's possible to land a dozen between 14 and 18 inches casting into the heads of pools, along shaded banks, and over drop-offs.

## Accommodations and Other Activities

The Hitching Post Motel (860-672-6219) is the only motel in Cornwall Bridge, but just south of the hamlet on Route 7 is the Cornwall Inn (800-786-6884) that has a restaurant open to the public on weekends and a small motel attached. To find other places to dine, anglers can travel seven miles west to Sharon, where they can eat at either the Country Corner Tavern, a family restaurant, or the West Main, located on the town's attractive village green. Or they can drive north to Canaan or south to Kent or to Bulls Bridge. My wife and I enjoy stopping for dinner at the Bulls Bridge Inn on the way home, although sometimes we drive north to Lakeville, or to neighboring Salisbury, to dine in one of their fine restaurants. There are two bed-and-breakfast inns in Cornwall, several miles east of Cornell Bridge, but they are very small. Hilltop Haven (860-672-8971) has nice views and two rooms while Cathedral Pines (860-672-6747) has one room.

Anglers can camp right on the river at Housatonic Meadows State Park (860-671-6772) or at one of two campgrounds nine miles south in Kent. Macedonia Brook State Park (860-927-4100) has lovely wooded campsites that run uphill alongside a brook trout stream that runs down from the mountain. Treetops Camp Resort (860-927-3555) is much larger, with 260 sites.

Hiking trails in the immediate area include the Mohawk Trail, which starts at Route 4 just north of Baird's, and the

*Ninety-year-old Chauncy Bales (standing) first fished the Hous in 1918.*

Pine Knob Loop Trail, which begins at a turnaround on Route 7 just north of the Sand Hole and immediately before a feeder creek at a bend in the road. It crosses the creek and meanders up the mountain. When hikers reach the top, they can see the river well below. The Appalachian Trail goes along the western side of the river for a brief period downstream from the no-kill section, but it can be accessed off Route 4 just west of its junction with Route 7.

The Housatonic Meadows State Park is a pleasant place where I leave Melody, who reads or does artwork while I fish. She also walks, accompanied by our two dogs, on the trail along the river's east side in West Cornwall that I referred to earlier. The state campground just up the road from the park has clean bathroom facilities where she can wash up for dinner.

When the river is high, family members might enjoy a trip on the river. Clark's Outdoors (860-672-6365), located just north of the state campgrounds, rents kayaks, canoes, and rafts and provides guided trips as well.

There are a few interesting stores in West Cornwall. They include the C. B. Pottery Store, Jan Ingersoll Shaker Furniture, that has hand-crafted furniture modeled after early Shaker furniture, a used-book store, and several snack bars. The Housatonic River Outfitters, a full-service fly shop, used to be located there, but the owner recently purchased a building directly across the street from Baird's Market in Cornell Bridge. Five miles west of Cornwall Bridge, on Route 4, is the Audubon Society. Their property includes pleasant walking trails around a small lake and the organization offers a variety of nature activities.

Those traveling north of West Cornwall to dine might want to hear the Music Mountain Chamber Music Festival (860-824-7126) that is held at Falls Village on weekends. It is the oldest continuously operated chamber music festival in the United States. The Housatonic Railroad Company (860-824-0339) runs a scenic trip along 17 miles of the river between Canaan and Cornwall Bridge. It runs on weekends from Memorial Day to the end of October.

The Village of Kent, nine miles downstream from Cornwall Bridge, has ice cream and frozen yogurt shops, antiques stores, gift shops, galleries, and several nice restaurants. Sidewalk sales are typical, especially book sales at the library. On the way to Kent from Cornwall Bridge, you pass Kent Falls State Park. The small park's main attractions are its waterfalls. Kent Falls Creek, which is within its boundaries, drops 200 feet in the park, with its longest waterfall being 70 feet. The creek is stocked with brook trout and it is an excellent place to teach children to fly-fish in the early spring. A trail borders the creek as it meanders from the top. I hiked it once to see if brook trout lived in its upper sections, but I didn't see any in the areas I examined. Above the park, the water is posted. They say there is good smallmouth fishing at the creek's junction with the Housatonic, but I have never tried it.

Two other creeks, Stewart Hollow Brook and Deep Brook, also enter the river near Kent Falls Creek, making the river water somewhat cooler in the summer than other sections of the river.

Anglers visiting Bull's Bridge, south of Kent, can cross over the covered bridge into New York and travel four miles to Webatuck Crafts Village in Wingdale, where Hunts Country Furniture has produced hand-crafted wooden furniture along the banks of the Ten Mile River since 1727. The Ten Mile is stocked with both small and large brown trout and I landed an 18-inch brown in the spring of 2003. My children enjoyed sitting in the oversized winged chair that stood at the entrance to the store. Prior to its construction, Bill O'Dell, an employee of the firm, built a 25-foot-tall, 14-foot-wide wooden chair in 1978 and placed it near the entrance to the village to promote the company. Shortly thereafter, it was listed in the *Guinness Book of World's Records*.

Unfortunately, the world's record holder was chopped down two years later after damage by vandals turned it into an eyesore. Sixteen years later, however, O'Dell erected a 28-foot, two-ton wooden chair and placed it by the store where it could be protected. Webatuck Trading, Toddle Time Toys, and the Buttonwood Café are situated next to Hunts.

# CHAPTER NINE

# Moosehead Lake Rivers
## *Landlocks in Primitive Waters*

Thoreau called Moosehead Lake, "A suitable wild looking sheet of water, sprinkled with low islands," and, "covered with shaggy spruce and other wild wood." Yet, Mt. Kineo, the lake's tallest island is far from a low island, towering 763 feet above the lake, with a west face that drops as a sheer cliff from top to bottom. And Moosehead Lake is rarely a sheet of water. Moosehead is Maine's largest freshwater lake, and when winds sweep over its 40-mile length and 117 square miles of water, it becomes downright inhospitable.

For several years, I traveled nine hours in the fall to fish for landlocked salmon in three rivers that adjoin the lake—the Moose, the Kennebec, and the Roach Rivers. The Moose flows out from a dam on Lake Brassua, and less than a mile below the dam its riffles, runs and pools turn into flat, deep water that must be fished from a boat. The Kennebec flows out of the lake's East Outlet and within three-and-one-half miles, enters Indian Pond. The Roach flows from the First Roach Pond, out the small Kokadjo dam, and enters the lake at Spencer Bay, about six miles downstream. I certainly didn't get tired hiking in to fish these three waters!

## Moosehead Lake

Although I came to fish the rivers, Moosehead Lake cannot be appreciated unless it is seen from the lake itself. The lake got its name not for the moose that inhabits its shores but for its shape. When map makers first looked at what they had drawn, they thought it resembled a Moose's head. On the first day of our three-day trip, Tom and I went out on the lake with a guide while Scott and Pete Mack, a former member of our fishing group, explored the area.

Our guide, Joe King, had lived in Maine's north woods all his life. He took us out from sunup to sundown, trolling in and out of coves while dozing at the outboard motor. If we were willing to put in a long day, so was he. Joe had guided a number of celebrities in his day, including either Chet Huntley or David Brinkley. The two famous television news anchormen were so inseparable that I can't remember which one Joe said he regularly guided. When Joe was younger, he worked for the lumber companies, but then found easier work traveling the carnival circuit and entering log rolling, tree climbing, and wood chopping contests and later performing these same activities in demonstrations sponsored by the timber community.

Almost anywhere on Moosehead Lake, you can't miss Mt. Kineo, located at the lake's waistline off the Village of Rockwood. It is an impressive chunk of green-tinged rock that erupted from the bowels of the earth more than 400 million years ago and later smoothed by glacial activity. Native Americans paddled out to the mountain to gather its volcanic stone, a flint-like rock easily made into weapons and gathering tools. They believed that the mountain was the petrified remains of a giant moose, sent to Earth by the Great Spirit to remind them that they could be punished similarly for their sins. Native Americans selected the lake as a place to settle because of the unique stones and the lakeside birch trees, whose bark they used to make canoes, shelters, and carryalls.

I love to watch the loons on the lake as our lines waver behind the boat. I consider them regal water birds, with their white necklace sharply contrasting with their all-black plumage. I think of each as a tuxedo bird, all dressed up with no place to go. The one I watched on this particular day was isolated against the backdrop of Big Squaw Mountain to the southwest. I could watch one loon for hours, guessing when and where it would come up each time it dove beneath the surface. I would much rather watch the loons than the seaplanes overhead transporting visitors into remote areas.

Dan Legere, owner of Maine Fly Fishing and Guide Service in Greenville, states that salmon caught trolling in the lake typically run between 14 and 16 inches, and that's exactly what we caught. It takes a landlock four years to reach 14 inches, so we were not catching young fish. Joe confirmed Dan's statements with "Yup, we don't often get big ones." As an afterthought, he added, "And when we do, you can be sure that the stories we tell about them grow and grow until our two-pounders become eight-pounders."

Joe said that lake trout can be caught between ten and 12 pounds, with an occasional larger one, but he didn't like trolling for them because you had to go deep, and after rising rapidly to the surface, unlike salmon that have an adjustable air bladder, their bladder would swell with air, causing them to die shortly after their release. But he did enjoy hooking the occasional brook trout near the surface because they usually weighed two to three pounds.

Trolling is a mindless, boring activity that calls for a rich imagination. I tried to imagine myself on the lake in my great grandfather's time. If there was no wind, I would have seen huge carrels of logs, perhaps two to five million feet of them at a time, covering acres of water, being drawn across the

*Mount Kineo, a mystifying mountain rising up from Maine's Moosehead Lake.*

lake by groups of lumbermen. The logs would be encased in a boom made from logs more than 30 feet long and firmly fastened end to end by chains attached to ropes. The ropes were passed through holes bored by auger and held together by what were called "thorough-shot" pins.

Once the boom had been closed around the logs, it was attached to the headworks by a short rope. The headworks was a small raft of hewn logs, attached to the carrel, upon which sat a huge spool made of a single log, called a capstan. The capstan revolved around a central shaft, drilled at the top to hold eight protruding bars of wood, called capstan bars. The whole contraption served as a winch, much like the winches that seamen pushed around to raise the sails on the old three-masted sailing ships. Attached to the capstan was 1,000 feet of inch-and-a-half rope that had been wound around it. The rope was so heavy that it took from ten to 15 men to coil it. At the rope's end was a huge anchor, weighing from 200 to 300 pounds. The anchor would be placed in a boat and

12 men would row it away from the headworks while four others would feed the rope from the spool.

When all the rope had been fed from the spool, the men would drop the anchor and row back to the headworks. Then, two men to a capstan bar, they would push on the bars while walking around and around the spool, winding the rope back onto it, and, in this fashion, draw the carrel of logs up to where the anchor had been dropped. The whole process was called warping and it was repeated over and over until the carrel had been drawn across the lake to the East Outlet, where river men would take the logs down the Kennebec River to the lumber mills.

If the lake was windy, particularly with a headwind, the whole vast circle of logs would be seen tied up at the shore, where the men would wait until the wind died down. A strong wind could blow the carrel back to where it had started from or even break up the carrel and the logs would float away. Because the lake was often windy, the carrels were usually moved at night, after the wind had died down. Men would walk round and round the capstan all night long. Some would fall asleep and still walk around, hypnotically stepping over the rope as it rose higher and higher on the capstan with each revolution. Lives could be lost working at night. The men would become careless from fatigue and fail to clear the rope as it moved higher on the spool, tripping over it and falling unnoticed by other drowsy workers into the lake's freezing-cold water.

In my grandfather's time, the man-powered rafts would have been replaced by steamships and we would have been surrounded by them as they towed carrels of logs across the lake. At the same time, other steamships would be taking sports, as wealthy fishermen were called in those days, to their Adirondack-style fishing clubs located along the lake's shore. Other sports built massive stone lodges. The fishing tales told by these sports put Moosehead on the tourist map. And several stream ships took visitors to the Mount Kineo Lodge, one of the largest hotels in America. At the peak of the season, some 50 steamers crossed and re-crossed the lake's waters. In the 1880s, visitors could take a train from New York to Bangor and then another from Bangor to Greenville Junction, a stone's throw from Greenville. In the 1900s, they could get on a Pullman Car in New York City in the evening and arrive in Greenville the next morning.

The following fall, we returned to the lake. Tom was anxious to put the boat to use that he had purchased in August. We found dock space at Rockwood Landing and, after a morning fishing the Moose river below Brassua Dam, we took it out into the lake. On the way up the river from the launch site to the lake, I hooked two small salmon casting from the bow. I thought the

easily-caught fish was a good omen for the day. As usual, they were not, as we only caught several more.

## The Moose River

After our day with Joe King, we fished Moose River the next morning. Between August 16 and September 30, the river can be fished only with flies and one fish can be kept. We accessed the river from the driveway owned by the Kennebec Water and Power Company and started fishing at the base of the Brassua Dam. Standing on a gravel bar, we cast well-leaded flies (split shot is illegal in Maine's fly-fishing-only waters) into the pool below the dam. While we didn't catch a salmon, we had the time of our lives, hooking, playing, and landing lake trout after lake trout, all 18 inches long and looking like they came from the same cookie cutter. You can imagine Scott's surprise when he also caught an 18-inch brook trout.

After lunch, Tom and I fished several hundred yards downstream from the dam just off Camp Road. Unlike the water running around the shallow gravel bar near the base of the dam, where plummeting water over the years had displaced gravel and widened the river, the water in this section was up to my waste as soon as I stepped off the bank. Quartering a Gray Ghost downstream, I realized that it sunk only an inch below the surface and yelled to Tom that we were wasting our time, but just as the words left my mouth, a salmon head appeared on the surface and grabbed my fly. The fish leaped several times on its way downstream and worked the strong current for all it was worth. I eventually brought it to the net. It was 19 inches.

Landlocked salmon are structurally the same as Atlantic salmon, with

*Landlocks, brookies and lakers gather in the fall at the base of Moose River's Brassua Dam waiting to be fooled on weighted streamers.*

slate-gray to black backs fading to bright silver sides, but landlocks typically have more black spots, although in some watersheds the two fish look almost identical. Studies suggest that stocked landlocks are no hardier than stocked trout, as less than 2% are caught by anglers. The Native Americans called the sea salmon "Pl-lahm" to distinguish it from the landlocked salmon which they called "Toy-e-wah-nahm." I have never fished for Atlantic salmon. Tom has, and his stories about the difficulty of landing these strong fish once they are hooked are fascinating.

Tom first fished for Atlantics on New Brunswick's famous Miramichi River. Before his heart troubles, Ted Williams fished the Miramichi every year after he retired from baseball. My father knew Ted and his favorite story about him is as follows. By letter, he invited Ted to speak at a dinner meeting of the Florida Chapter of the Sears Roebuck Retirees Association and added that he could bring a guest. Later, my father realized that he had neglected to mention in his letter to Ted that the dinner was a formal affair. He knew that Ted wouldn't care. As the guest speaker, he could dress any way he pleased, but he knew that Ted's wife would care. When he tried to call Ted the operator informed him that the number was unlisted and could not be given out. Desperate, my father explained the situation to the female operator and asked her how she would feel if she came dressed informally to a formal party. Since he put it that way, the operator promised that she, personally, would call Mrs. Williams and leave her the message that the dinner was formal. Pop thanked her profusely. Ted arrived at the dinner, but instead of his wife, he brought his fishing guide!

Atlantic salmon spend their adult lives in the ocean and run up coastal rivers to spawn. Landlocks, unless the river in which they live is below a lake, spend their adult lives in a lake, originally in lakes cut off from the sea by geological upheaval. They run up the lake's tributaries in the fall to spawn.

Because they do not usually feed during their spawning run, fishing for landlocks and Atlantics in rivers is like fishing for shad—you have to repeatedly cast over a suspected lie with the hope that the spawning fish will strike out of instinct. Nevertheless, unlike Pacific salmon, they will sometimes rise to the dry fly.

Tom entered the Moose River farther downstream from me, having seen a splashy rise, and he put on a caddis. Wading out into the fast water, farther then I would dare to venture, he struggled against the strong current, but he gradually got within casting distance of where the fish had splashed. He cast his line behind him and then abruptly stopped his forward cast at 11 o'clock, the fly landed several yards in front of him, and he fluttered it as it floated downstream to the spot where the fish last rose. There was a big splash, followed by a bent rod, and a large salmon leaping several times more than did

mine on its way downstream. After netting the fish, Tom walked downstream in search of another rising fish. I eased into the river again, cast across the current, let the fly swing with a tight line, and retrieved the fly in rapid jerks upstream. Stepping down river, I repeated the whole process. I did this for about an hour, but I had no further hits, nor was Tom witness to another rise.

When we returned to Moosehead Lake the following fall, work was being done on the Brassua Dam, the Moose River was low, and few salmon were running up from the lake. I took one 17-inch salmon floating a hair-winged caddis down a shallow riffle past a log held fast to a rock by the current. The fish came out from under the log, grabbed the fly, and cartwheeled downstream, but that was it. We thought about fishing the Moose between Long Pond and Little Brassua Lake. It is big water with huge boulders, large riffles, and long runs and it

*Tom Royster casting a caddis to a rising landlock on Maine's Moose River.*

can be easily accessed from a side road off Highway 6/15, along the Canadian-American Railroad tracks, or at a road that crosses over the river about halfway between the pond and the lake. Instead, we decided to fish the lake from Tom's boat.

Residents fished for landlocks on Maine's rivers well before the Civil War. In the late 1860s, a small group of residents became concerned about the increasing harvest of landlocks, the loss of their spawning grounds to siltation, and the multiplication of barriers that blocked the landlocks' efforts to reach the few remaining spawning grounds. Stimulated by the works of the Treat brothers who had enclosed a section of a stream in Eastport, Maine for cultivation of Atlantic Salmon eggs, Maine's fisheries commissioners embarked on a landlocked salmon stocking program. Salmon were captured from Grand Lake Stream, a tributary to the West Branch of the St. Croix River, at the outlet of West Grand Lake during the spawning season of 1867. Reverend William Clift later established a landlocked salmon hatchery on the Grand Lake Stream. In December of 1868, 8,000 eyed salmon eggs were packed in gauze bags, placed in a tin box lined with sphagnum, and driven to a private hatchery in Manchester where the eggs were hatched and the fry raised. The salmon fry were then put into Mill Stream, a tributary to Cathance Lake that feeds the Dennys River, a small river on Maine's northern coast.

## The Kennebec River

Starting at the East Outlet dam, we fished down the Kennebec to Indian Pond. All we got was one tiny salmon. Although a big river, the Kennebec is extremely clear in this section because settled lake water is what enters it.

Walking along the bank and inspecting the clear water, we didn't see a single large fish. We worked the more turbulent waters just below the outlet, considered a hot spot by locals, when we first arrived and again when we left, but with no success.

There were no good ole days on the Kennebec River, or any of Maine rivers for that matter, except for the netting of Atlantic salmon to feed the logging crews in the early 1800s. The Atlantic salmon disappeared following the forest industries' dams, log-holding ponds, and water-powered mills. Following the lumber industry, the rivers had been reserved for years for the paper companies, thereby limiting public access. The paper companies returned the privilege by choking them with logs and poisoning them with yellow bile that one historian said "smelled like a boiled New England dinner gone bad." Sport fishing in Maine's rivers took off after log drives were banned in 1976. In essence, my companions and I were fishing the Kennebec River in the good ole days.

Some anglers fished Maine's rivers in the months following the major lumber drives, but most were polluted from bark deposits, sunken pulpwood, and sawdust. Many tributary streams were bulldozed to facilitate the pulpwood drives. Some streams became flattened ditches when their protective cover was removed, their loops and turns straightened, and their narrow sections widened and flattened for pulpwood landings. The decomposition of sawdust and bark robbed the rivers of oxygen and no fish could live long in stretches of them. Some rivers were so polluted with the sawdust, chloride of lime, and vitriol oil dumped into the rivers by the paper industry that their waters were unfit even for paper processing. And if that wasn't enough, starch factories bordering the rivers dumped organic waste directly into them and DDT spraying, to protect spruce trees from bud worm infestations, poisoned them.

When men were still lumbering on the Kennebec, the more daring river runners would ride a log down a sluiceway and into the river. In fact, a movie producer once came to the river with the intention of shooting a picture of a man riding a log down a sluiceway. When his stunt man saw what would be required of him, he refused to do it. Undaunted, the movie maker inquired around town and the locals told him that Spider Ellis, one of the Kennebec's best log men, would be the man for the job. He located Ellis and offered him $5 to ride a log down a dam sluiceway. Ellis accepted the offer, after all, two days' wage for two minutes of fun was an opportunity that didn't often come along.

The movie maker then offered Ellis $10 if he would ride another log, but this time he asked Ellis to fall off the log and into the white water below the dam. Ellis took the money in advance, but after he rode the log down the sluiceway and out into the river, he was still standing on it. The movie producer confronted him about this insubordination and Ellis replied, "You see, I have never fallen off a log in my life. I find I just can't fall off one for less than $25!"

## The West Branch of the Penobscot

On our second trip to the area, we went to the West Branch of the Penobscot. The West Branch drains 2,000 square miles while flowing 200 miles from its headwaters at the Canadian border to its junction with the East Branch at Medway. While a

lumber road from Rockwood was the fastest way to reach the section we planned to fish, this road was closed, requiring us to take Lily Bay Road north, where we passed Lily Bay State Park, a nearly 1,000-acre park, where visitors gather to see moose feeding on the water plants growing in a bog near the Mud Bank picnic area.

We took Lily Bay Road for about 23 miles until we reached the Bowater/Great Northern's Sias Hill Checkpoint, paid our $8, and took Telos Road until we hit the Golden Road that would take us west to the river. We went for what seemed like forever on both these isolated dirt roads owned by the Great Northern Paper Company, who built them in the 1970s. As we drove on and on, the only change in scenery from the tall pines was the red and white mile markers, and they, too, became monotonous. Repeatedly, we had to squeeze close to the roadside when the lumber trucks came roaring down the road, kicking up so much dust we couldn't see to drive.

We fished the West Branch at Hannibal's Crossing, a section of the river just north of Moosehead's North Bay. The river flows out of the dam on Seboomook Lake and then northward to Chesuncook Lake. I do not remember a bridge at the crossing so the outlet at the dam must have been regulated to enable the lumber trucks to drive right through the riverbed. After a brief inspection we realized that this section was best fished from a boat. We saw several canoes on the opposite shoreline, beached at what looked like a riverside campsite, awaiting their owner's return and we wished we could make use of them.

I rigged up and cast a streamer across and downstream, but a short way downstream the river deepened and I could wade no farther, nor could I hike up and over a cliff that impeded my progress. Putting on a dry fly, I fished my way back up to the car, catching several small salmon on the way. Tom stayed near the car, having found a point of land where he could stand on a rock and cast dry flies into a riffle. He lost one salmon about 17 inches, but had no other hits. Scott didn't fare much better so we left to fish the Roach in the evening. Later, we learned that we should have taken a lumber road, just south of Golden Road, that ran along the river and then fished in the two-mile section southwest of Hannibal's Crossing or at the base of the dam.

Initially, we had planned to travel further north on Telos Road to fish the famed West Branch of the Penobscot in the section that flows from the Ripogenus Dam at Chesuncook's outlet to the Nesowadnebunk Dead Water. The Ripogenus Dam was first built around 1920 to store water for driving logs downriver to Great Northern's paper mills at Millinocket and later used to generate electricity to power the mills. Although the river is primarily nursery water for young salmon, mature salmon follow the spring smelt run upriver from the Pemadumcook chain of lakes below. In June, the population of salmon in the river greatly decreases, even though some smelt, washed down from Chesuncook Lake, remain in the river all year. In the fall, mature salmon return to the river to spawn. Fishing opportunities on the West Branch significantly increased in 1972 with the end of Great Northern's pulpwood drives and it was from that year forward that the river earned its reputation.

Unfortunately, we did not fish it on this trip because close to 3,000 cubic feet of water were rushing from the dam's outlet, a volume of water loved by rafters, but not by fishermen. Years ago, no fishermen would dare to fish the West Branch in the spring because the river's sole purpose was to transport logs. There has never been a log-driving river equal to the West Branch of the Penobscot. In the 1860s, Bangor processed 200 million board feet of lumber a year, with most of it transported by the waters of the West Branch. In the river's lower harbors, 3,000 ships waited to take the lumber to ports throughout the world.

Prior to 1825, after the breakup of ice in the spring, every lumberman who had cut logs over the winter started to drive his logs down the Penobscot to Old Town and Bangor. The earlier one's logs were on their way in the early season high water, the quicker they arrived at their destinations. All winter long the logs accumulated by the riverside in immense skidways, stretching for miles along the river. Loggers had to go below the huge skids and loosen the wedges that held the logs in place, scrambling for safety as the logs tumbled into the river. If the winter snow had been light and there was insufficient water in the river, log jams were more frequent and log jams made more widows than did hung-up trees.

A jam started when one log got hung up on a boulder in the river and other logs got caught on this key log. Log jams grew up the length of the river, rather than across it, unless they were created in a narrow section. To prevent jams, drivers were positioned at strategic corners or out in the river on rocks known to create jams. The men stood for hours, deflecting logs with a ten-foot pike, called a "peavey." "High bankers" were those who tended easy stretches of river, while "road monkeys" were those accorded more respect because they tended more difficult sections. But "riders" were the most respected because they floated down the river's edge on a fat log, poking and prodding the shore-bound stragglers, occasionally engaging in the dangerous game of "burling," or trying to knock another man off his log.

But jams occurred in spite of preventive measures. The foreman of each crew volunteered a modest group of men to take their pikes, axes, and dynamite sticks, get into a jam boat, and row out to the jam. Their task was to find the key log and then chop at it slowly, listening for log shifting to take place. If shifting was heard, the men would dash across the logs to the boat and the oarsman would row frantically to avoid getting caught in the tangled mess that followed when the shifting broke up the jam and the logs started to flow. Sometimes the logs stopped moving, so the second attempt typically involved the use of dynamite, an even more dangerous method. But eventually the logs would be freed, even at the cost of lives, and they would proceed down the river to their destinations.

Most of these drives occurred at the same time. As a result, the logs of the different owners needed sorting when they arrived at their destinations. Crews in boats worked all day and night at this task. Huge bonfires were built along the shore to create light so the workers could see their unique mark on the logs as they floated by. Nevertheless, in the dim light, many logs floated past the workers and were lost at sea.

The Penobscot is no longer congested with logs. It is now congested with rafts. The New England Outdoor Center recently built a huge complex on the eastern outskirts of Millinocket, easily reached off Interstate 95, and rafters, kayakers, and canoeists endlessly float the river, distracting from the solitude needed for a satisfying fishing experience. Two numbers can be called to obtain information on water releases (207-695-3756 or 800-322-9844), controlled by the Bowater/ Great Northern Paper Company, and if the water is high do not make the trip.

The first summer after Maine prohibited transportation of logs and pulpwood down the state's rivers, Wayne Hockemeyer and a small group of close friends took a crude raft down the Kennebec River and white water rafting in Maine began. Hockemeyer was the first to open a rafting company, called Northern Outdoors, closely followed by Jim Ernst, a white-water rafting guide from Colorado, who opened Maine Whitewater, and by Jim Connely, a guide from West Virginia, who opened Eastern River Expeditions. Today, numerous white water rafting companies serve some 60,000 people who raft Maine's rivers each summer, all featuring trips on the Dear, Kennebec, and West Branch of the Penobscot, with the Penobscot preferred because large releases from the Ripogenus Dam are the norm rather than the exception.

## The Roach River

After the seemingly long return from the West Branch, we arrived at the Roach about five o'clock, leaving us with only about an hour of daylight left in which to fish. Tom decided to fish just below the small Kokadjo Dam at the outlet to First Roach Pond. Scott took off downstream, and I entered the river just west of Lily Bay Road. The river in this stretch was narrow and shallow, lined with overhanging bushes, some of which grew in the streambed and required my squirming through them. But worst of all, the section was devoid of holding water. I tossed a streamer against the banks as I worked downstream, knowing full well that no fish were there to strike it. I quit at the mouth of Lazy Tom Creek and returned to see how Tom was doing near the dam. He hadn't turned a fish.

It was now dark and Scott had not returned. We began to worry, so I went looking for him. I stumbled my way downstream in the riverbed, where I could see him if he had fallen, and called for him, but the roar of the current drowned out my voice. I then wondered if he had unknowingly passed by me, returning to the car on some path north of the river where the stream-side bushes would have blocked his view of me. Nevertheless, when I arrived at the car, Tom, who had looked for him along a discovered path, reported that he still hadn't returned. Now we were really perplexed. I thought that Scott had slipped on the rocks, fallen in the river, and hit his head. I visualized his body floating down the fast current and out into the lake. How would I explain this to his wife, Karen? "Didn't we keep tabs on each other?" she would scream in anguish.

But just then, Scott appeared, through the darkness, looking like a ghost. I was never so relieved! A short distance below the car he discovered a footpath on the river's north bank and had walked down it until he heard the voices of other fishermen. Because ours was the only car parked off Lily Bay Road, we assumed we were alone on the river, not realizing until later that anglers can access the river from other spots. They can park at several locations along two lumber roads owned by the Scott Paper Company and take paths from the road to the river or they can access it from Casey's Spencer Bay Campgrounds, located on the lake shore just north of the creek.

Two anglers were fishing in a deep hole where large brook trout were feeding on the surface. Scott watched one angler lose a fish and when he left in disgust, his friend joined him, and Scott waded in to take his place. But the big fish were just out of the range of his roll cast and by then it was too dark for him to see. As he waded out of the hole, he could still hear the slurping noises of these big feeding fish.

## Other Seasons on Moosehead's Rivers

I have never fished Moosehead's rivers in the spring, but those who have seem to prefer the spring over the fall, perhaps because they catch more fish at this time. Shortly after ice-out, smelt run up the rivers to spawn and the salmon follow them, where, preoccupied with sex rather than survival, the smelt are easily captured. Anglers fishing in the early spring make less use of traditional smelt patterns, like the Gray Ghost I used, and choose from among the newer patterns, such as Joe's Smelt, Umbagog Smelt, or Harry's Krystal Special, developed by Harry Vanderweide of Augusta, Maine. Joe's Smelt is tied with pearl Mylar piping for the body because pearl best duplicates the flash of the spawning hues of smelt.

During the rest of the season, salmon often move into the rivers from the lakes after heavy rains and stonefly patterns are effective in hooking them. Some mature salmon dwell in the West Branch of the Penobscot all season long and anglers fish for them as they would for trout, except that salmon

*Each fall the short stretch below Moose River's Brassua Dam*
*gives up a number of landlocked salmon.*

prefer large riffles and long holes over the tight places that trout usually frequent.

## Accommodations and Other Activities

Anglers who want to be equidistant from the Moosehead and Roach Rivers can stay in Greenville, a town at the Lake's south end that was established in 1836 and is now the corporate center for the lumber companies. Inexpensive motels include the Greenwood Hotel (800-477-4386), a two-story 15-room establishment, and the Chalet Moosehead Lake-Front Motel (800-290-3645), a two-story motel that has its own private sandy beach as well as an attached restaurant. More upscale, is the Blair Hill Inn (207-695-0024), perched on a hill overlooking the lake. Kelly's Landing, with indoor and outdoor dining on the waterfront, is a good place to eat for those staying in

Greenville. Those who travel with pets can check-in at the Indian Hill Motel (800-771-4620), a typical one-story motel with 15 rooms, or at the Kineo View Motor Lodge (800-659-8439), three miles south of Greenville, located on a hilltop with a good view of Mt. Kineo.

Bed-and-breakfast inns include the Devlin House (207-695-2229), an inn with the same view of the lake as the more expensive Moosehead Lake Lodge, Pleasant Street Inn (207-695-2229), and Lakeview House (207-695-3543), an 1897 Victorian restored in 1997. Anglers with deep pockets can choose the Lodge at Moosehead Lake (207-695-4400) off Lily Bay Road, or at the Greenville Inn (888-695-6000). The lodge has five guest rooms and three bi-level carriage house suites. The five rooms are named Bear, Loon, Moose, Totem, and Trout, with all but Trout having dramatic views of the lake. The

*A silver-bright landlocked salmon from Moose River.*

Greenville Inn is a gray-blue 1895 Victorian that was once a lumber baron's lake house. It has five second-story suites, a rustic carriage house suite, six cottages with mountain views, and an attached restaurant. Neither inn takes pets.

Those anglers concentrating their efforts on the Roach can lodge at the Northern Pride Lodge (207-695-2890) at First Roach Pond, the 1896 home of a former lumber magnate. Its owner, Jeff Lucas, is a fly-fisherman well acquainted with the rivers. West Branch Ponds (207-695-2561), near Kokadjo, has eight shoreline cabins on First West Branch Pond, but it is ten miles east of Lily Bay Road. The Kokadjo Trading Post, the last outpost before entering the North Woods, is located above the hamlet with the same name. It is near Lazy Tom Bog, off the Scott Paper Company road just north of the Roach River.

Campers fishing the Roach typically choose one of the 15 campsites at Casey's Spencer Bay Camps (207-695-2801) or one of the 93 sites at Lily Bay State Park (207-287-3824), where a number of sites are on the waterfront. A two-night minimum stay is required and advance reservations should be made during July and August. Those who enjoy wilderness camping can choose from among the free campsites maintain by the Maine Forest Service (207-695-3721), although many are accessible only by boat. *Colmon's Guide to National Forest Service Campgrounds* can be consulted by those planning a primitive camping venture.

In Rockwood, a hamlet 20 miles northeast of Greenville, the Moosehead Motel (207-545-7787) has an attached restaurant that serves breakfast and dinner. Boats can be rented at the harbor across the way. Small cottages on the west shore include the Abnaki Housekeeping Cottages (207-534-7318), Mt. Kineo Cabins (207-534-7744), Rockwood Cottages (207-534-7725), and Sundown Cabins

(207-534-7357). The cabins where we stayed, the Old Mill Campground and Cabins, may no longer operate, at least not under that name, although there is still a listing for the campgrounds (207-534-7373). The Birches Resort (800-825-9453), the most expensive, has four rooms in its main lodge and 15 rustic cabins. It includes a dining room open to the public and moose-sighting cruises. Anglers planning to fish the Moose River above Little Lake can camp at the Moose River Campground (207-668-3341) in Jackman or stay at the Attean Lake Lodge (207-668-3792), an island lodge on Attean Pond. Both are about an hour west of Rockwood.

Anglers fishing the storied section of the West Branch below the Ripogenus dam often camp at Pray's Big Eddy Wilderness Campground (297-723-9581) which overlooks the rock-choked Crib Works Rapids, a Class V rapid rafted by only the bravest. The campground is located just north of the Telos Road bridge over the river. The Abol Bridge Campground is also on the river. Two other campsites are located along Baxter State Park Road—the Forest Pond Camps (207-885-4488) and the Hidden Springs Campground (888-885-4480), with the later having sites on a lake. Overnight camping is allowed in Baxter State Park (207-723-5140) by reservation only, in lean-to shelters. The park contains a number of hiking trails, ranging in distance from one-and-a-half miles to ten miles. Canoes can be rented at the South Branch Pond. The Seboomook Wilderness Campgrounds (201-534-8824), located 28 unpaved miles north of Rockwood, offers 28 campsites for those fishing the Penobscot below Seboomook Dam.

From the dock at Rockwood Landing, lake cruises can be taken which include a stopover at Mt. Kineo, on either the 48-foot Socatean, operated by Jolly Roger's Moosehead Cruises (207-574-8827), or the Katahdin, a restored steamship operated by Katahdin Cruises (207-695-2716), which is affiliated with the Moosehead Marine Museum. The museum features exhibits of former logging activities and of the steamship era and displays old photos of the last log drive and of the former Mount Kineo Hotel. Both cruise ships offer three-hour-plus cruises, although on Thursdays the Katahdin offers a six-and-one-half-hour cruise.

The Kino Launch runs back and forth continuously from the public landing at Rockwood to Mt. Kineo for a cost of around $3. The Rockwood Cottages also operates a shuttle on demand for about $5. By renting a boat at Rockwood landing, you can take yourself to Mt. Kineo and within 15 minutes you can be sipping a drink at the tavern that operates on the island.

The home of the Moosehead Historical Society, the Eevleth-Crafts-Sheridan House on Main Street in Rockwood, is a nineteenth-century building displaying the region's history, Native American artifacts, and other items of historical interest. It is also the birthplace of a melancholy story of unrequited love that I won't tell you should you visit the museum.

Those planning to fish the classic waters of the West Branch of the Penobscot below the Ripogenus Dam and to visit Baxter State Park, a 300-square-mile forever wild state park just north of the river where the Appalachian Trail ends, would do well to purchase Stephan Clark's *Katahdin: A Guide to Baxter State Park and Katahdin*.

# CHAPTER TEN

# New York's Salmon River
## *A River in Transition*

The first time I saw the Salmon River, a river that flows into Lake Ontario south of the Town of Pulaski, I never thought I'd cast a line into its black waters. Every September since 1970, my companions and I passed over the river on our way to fish for bass and pike in New York's Thousand Islands. The river looked like a good trout stream below the highway where we crossed over it. It originated from the southwest edge of Tug Hill Plateau and it drained close to 300 square miles of the western Adirondacks. What puzzled us, however, was that on our way to the Thousand Islands it was roaring along, and on our return three days later it was just a trickle.

We stopped once in Pulaski to inquire about the river and learned that its waters above Pulaski had been empty of trout ever since the Niagra Mohawk Power Company built the Lighthouse Hill Reservoir and the dam at Altmar, about 17 miles from the river's mouth at Lake Ontario. Releases from the dam subjected the river to dramatically varying water flows. In the late summer and fall months, it could be walked across in certain sections without getting your feet wet. As a result, it was without both plant and insect life. Trout were now confined to sections well above the reservoir.

In the early 1980s, we heard that chinook, also called Pacific or king salmon, and coho salmon had been stocked in Lake Ontario from a newly built fish hatchery on the Salmon River and that they had grown large in the lake and were now fair game for anglers during their September and early October return to the river. At one time, Lake Ontario supported the largest population of lake-dwelling

118

Atlantic salmon known to man and the Salmon River was so thick with them in the fall that early settlers named the river after them. By 1900 they had vanished. Today, the Salmon River Fish Hatchery in Altmar, New York, raises annually, three million plus chinook salmon, one quarter of a million coho salmon, three quarters of a million steelhead, 300,000 brown trout, and 150,000 Atlantic salmon.

We wondered how the salmon navigated the Salmon River when the water was low, so we stopped at its mouth on our way home from the Thousand Islands to see the run for ourselves. The mouth, however, was not the place to view the run because the river there was too deep to see any fish that might be moving upriver. While at the mouth, we talked to a gentleman who reported that the run had started and added that a poacher had dynamited the river just last night and had poached a number of early running salmon. The man didn't seem particularly concerned, however, "After all," he said, "they die after they spawn anyway, and the damn things don't belong in this river." We then drove up to the village of Pulaski and, in response to our inquires, one bystander replied, "You don't see any fishermen here today because it is Sunday, the power company is holding back water at the dam at Altmar, and the salmon are waiting at the river's mouth for more water before they run up the river. On Monday, when the region needs more power, water will be released from the dam and there will be so many salmon in the river that you won't believe it! Hundreds of anglers, who take days off in September, or don't work, will be lining the banks and casting to these huge fish."

I asked, "What happens to the fish when they are in the river and the water is held back?"

He said, "They drop down into the bigger holes, such as the School House Pool, Trestle Pool, Sportsman Pool, and the Black Hole, where they are sitting ducks for snaggers."

"But how do they spawn?" I asked.

"They don't," he said. "Those reaching the hatchery runways at Altmar are stripped of their roe and sperm by DEC staff, the roe is fertilized artificially, the eggs hatch in the hatchery pens, and the fry are transferred to start tanks and then raised in smolt ponds. Some are then released from the ponds into the river while others are transported to tributaries or placed directly into harbors or into Lake Ontario."

## Crickets, Crickets, and More Crickets

The next fall we stopped in Pulaski and although it was Sunday, water was being released from the dam following a period of heavy rain. Anglers were lined up like cancan dancers along the river's banks. On one side of the river, anglers stood elbow to elbow on a retaining wall about 20 feet above the river. When they snagged a fish, they walked downstream along the narrow wall, worked their way around other anglers, climbed down the wall on its west end, and fought the fish on the riverbank below. Sometimes an angler would slip in his haste to follow the fish downstream, and fall off the wall into the river. Some were seriously injured.

It was like watching an old Three Stooges movie. With short, stiff rods, star-drag reels fitted with 40-pound-test lines, a line of anglers would cast treble hooks with their shanks encased in lead, called "crickets," from one side of the river to the other. They retrieved the crickets in jerks until they snagged a salmon. Almost every angler snagged one while we were watching. When more water was released and the fish dispersed more, less fish were snagged, but even then most anglers landed their two-fish limit from this relatively narrow river.

As a fish catapulted downstream, anglers would frantically reel in their lines. Those fishermen standing just below the fish-fighting angler couldn't possibly reel fast enough, having to duck if the angler when behind them or to lower their rods so the angler could step over their lines if going in front of them. Those whose lines became entangled with the fighting angler's line had to rapidly strip line from their reels or cut their line because if their lines remained taut the fish would break off, angering the fighting angler. Many anglers fell several times on the slippery rocks as they made their way down the river. When the fish wasn't landed fast enough, waiting anglers would get angry and sometimes cut the line of the struggling angler so they could return to fishing. If cross-stream anglers didn't hook each other's lines, they would often snag the same poor fish and angry shouting would ensue.

We sat on the bank and laughed hysterically at the antics of these fishermen, although when we stopped and thought about it, we realized that the situation was distressing. Anglers, who were probably sportsmen at other times, had regressed to being rude ruffians. We witnessed anglers taking their two fish to coolers in their cars and then coming back for more.

Several years later I learned that a neighbor fished Pulaski's salmon run every fall and that he used wet flies. I asked him how he dealt with the cricket slingers who lined the river. He told

*A line of Salmon River fishermen waiting for a chinook run in the village of Pulaski.*

me he went with two carloads of friends, arrived at the river early each morning, and staked out a stretch just above Black Hole, a spot that was not particularly popular with snaggers because it was a long, shallow rapid. He and his friends would space themselves along the rapids, expecting most of the fish to ignore the flies of the lower anglers as they moved upstream through the rapids and be hooked by the angler at the head of the rapids. When the upstream angler followed his hooked fish on its run downstream, the second angler would move upstream to the spot just vacated by the first angler. The last angler in line would net the first angler's fish in the Black Hole and then hand the net to the first angler who would take his place. He said that this was how groups fished for salmon in European waters. I pondered this information, but decided that even fly-fishing for these big salmon just didn't excite me. There were so many fish in the river that, to me, fly-fishing was just another form of snagging.

Driving along the river, we came upon a number of small shacks advertising that they smoked salmon for a fee and purchased salmon roe. We now understood why our earlier informant had stressed "don't work" when referring to some of the anglers. For many years, Pulaski had been an economically depressed area and by selling salmon roe some of the unemployed could make some spending money. After all, caviar is an expensive delicacy. Years ago, smoke houses existed along the river to smoke other migrating fish. Weirs were built across lake Ontario rivers to trap eels, which were then smoked and shipped downstate for sale. At the peak of the late nineteenth century, about 1,000 barrels of a smoked eel were shipped from Lake Ontario's rivers to New York City each year. Eels had always been an important food in Europe, so much so that fines were often paid in eels rather than in money.

We were informed that some of the roe was made into spawn sacks, frozen, and sold as bait later in the year when steelhead ran up the river to spawn. The state also stocked steelhead in the Salmon River and the initial spawning runs back from the lake had been unexpectedly large. Unlike casting for salmon, where snagging was legal, the snagging of steelhead was forbidden so anglers used the spawn sacks to catch them.

## Lines of "Lifters"

With pressure from environmentally-oriented anglers, the snagging of salmon was eventually limited on the river to the waters downstream from the Route 2A bridge over the river, the first bridge east of Route 81, and lifting was allowed upstream from the bridge. By definition, lifting is fishing with a single-baited hook to which is attached a weight no less than 18 inches from the hook. In addition, only fish hooked in the mouth could be kept. If hooked elsewhere, they were illegally caught, or snagged, and were supposed to be returned to the river.

On our next trip to Thousand Islands, we stopped to watch the lifters working below the second bridge above Route 81 where lifting was legal. Our initial impression was that lifting was more sporting than snagging. Lifting was like short line, or short-stick nymphing. Anglers were out in the river, usually waste deep in order to reach the main channel, flipping their lines up and slightly across stream. Lifters would watch their lines float by and down below them and, if it hesitated or stopped, they sharply lifted their rod tips and perhaps found their line attached to a fish. Hooked this way, the fight of the salmon was more spectacular than when it was snagged on its side by a heavy cricket.

But when we watched a lifter closely, we saw that the lift was actually a jerk. Normally, when a baited hook floats into the body of a big salmon holding in the slower bottom current, the current eventually pushes it around the fish and it floats farther downstream. But with lifting, it does not pass by the disinterested salmon because as soon as it touches the fish, it is jerked upward by the angler. This upward jerk snags the fish, sometimes in the mouth because salmon and trout continually open and close their mouths while swimming, but just as often elsewhere. Bait on the hook was really not needed because the salmon wasn't the least bit interested in it. Everybody knew that the salmon didn't really try to eat the bait, especially the state biologists, yet the rules were set and the game was played as if fish actually fed on the egg affixed up the hook shank so as not to interfere with the snagging. True, lifting took more skill than snagging, but it was still not fishing.

## Current Regulations

After many years, snagging with crickets ended. Regulations were instituted that required free-swinging hooks and forbade the use of trebled-hook lures that sank, but they were replaced by another form of snagging, a form that resulted in lifters switching to a new technique even though lifting is still legal, but much more difficult to accomplish. The use of hooks with added weights is now prohibited, except that artificial flies with no more than 1/8 ounce added weight can be used. Anglers in Alaska use a technique where the Glo Bug is placed far above the hook, but Salmon River lifters are not likely to use this technique when they can more easily use a floating lure that dives.

Scott and I stopped at the Salmon in the fall of 1999 and watched anglers on the river in several different sections. We saw no lifters anywhere. All anglers, except those in the fly-fishing only sections, were snagging salmon using a method almost identical to the original snagging technique with crickets. The state, in its infinite wisdom, now allows the use of floating lures. Today, snaggers toss a large crank bait,

fitted with wide-gapped hooks, that dive once it is reeled in and then they jerk the lure as they reel it across the bottom of the river. Lifting took more skill!

While the majority of anglers simply want to hook and land a big salmon, Farmington, Connecticut resident Nunzio Incremona, has learned how to make salmon fishing more sporting. Using a fly rod and two-pound-test tippet, he landed a 26-pound, 38-inch coho salmon and a 25 pound, 37-inch chinook salmon on a No. 6 pink and a No. 6 yellow Comet fly. Both of these fish were two-pound-test world's records. Three hours after Incremona released both fish they were caught again upstream by two fishermen who had witnessed his catch.

Records are not new to Incremona. He has been catching salmon on light tippets since the early 1990s. After establishing the six-pound tippet line class world's record, with a 24-pound, seven-ounce chinook, set in 1995, he switched to two-pound-test tippet, and in 1996 he landed a 24-pound, 36-inch chinook, the former world's record for this line class. He set both records in the Salmon River. Other world salmon records set the Salmon River include a 30-pound coho, taken on 20-pound-test line, set in 1985, and a 33-pound coho, caught on 30-pound-test line, set in 1989. The latter is also the current Great Lakes record coho. The current Great Lakes record chinook, also caught in the Salmon River, is 47 pounds.

Incremona notes that "In Alaska (where the other line class records are held), most record fish are hooked when they are dark and tired, at the end of their life. Part of the thrill of catching record breaking fish here (on the Salmon) is that you hook them when they're strong, young, and chrome silver."

## Steelhead

Intrigued by reports of winter steelhead fishing in the Salmon River, we decided to give it a try. On our first trip, on a Thanksgiving in the early 1980s, we learned that the steelhead were caught only during the brief period when the water was first released from the dam at Altmar. After the released water reached the lake, the river remained high all day and the fishing was poor. To generate electricity for area residents, water was released from the dam about seven o'clock in the morning. Parking ourselves at either the School House or Trestle Pools, the first good holes below the dam, we waited for the release, and for the river to rise, and then began our fishing.

As the river rose, the steelhead began feeding, but as soon as the water reached a certain level they stopped. When this occurred, we would scurry back up the trail to our car, drive downstream to the Sportsman's or Compactor pools, wait for the released water to come to it, and begin fishing again. In this manner, we drove from hole to hole until the water reached the lake and then we quit the river for the day. From about 6:30 until 10:30 in the morning, if we preceded the flowing water downstream, we could fish for steelhead.

The release of water was believed to stir up the eggs of those salmon who tried to spawn. The steelhead then fed on these eggs until the high water washed them downstream and away from the fish. I never bought this theory. If it were true, all the salmon eggs would be gone from the river after several days of releases. I believed that the high and fast flowing water made it

impossible to get the bait down deep enough and for it to move slow enough to interest the fish who stayed right on the bottom. No fish will expend more energy capturing drifting eggs than the energy they derive from eating them. For this reason, fishing was most successful when the water first rose, a time when the fish moved upriver from their holding spots and when the fishermen could keep their bait on the bottom.

When the river got high, we would fish the feeder creeks, Trout Brook, Orwell Brook, and John O'Hara Brook. We never landed the fish we hooked in these little creeks because they were choked with fallen tress and held huge boulders. But it sure was exciting to hook a ten-pound fish in a brook trout stream, climbing over and straddling trees while you fought it. Sometimes the fish ran up onto the bank before they broke off! If there were no fish in the feeder creeks, we went back to our motel and waited until the next morning or, if they weren't frozen over, we fished the smaller streams along Route 3, north of Pulaski, such as the North and South Sandy Creeks.

Tom and I both caught our first steelhead in North Sandy Creek. We fished it before we ever fished the Salmon because our first trip to Pulaski was on a weekend and water was not being released from the dam at Altmar. We parked along the road and walked through the fields to a spot some distance upstream from our car. Using a spawn sack, Tom worked his way farther upstream and was rounding a bend in the creek when his line hesitated on its drift downstream. He set the hook, and a steelhead broke the surface. I missed this inaugural event because I had walked back to the car to replace a faulty reel.

When I got within earshot of Tom on my return, he yelled that the fish hit just after I left for the car and that it was too big to land in his trout net. Would I go back to the car and get our pike net? He assured me that the fish had plenty of fight left in it and that it wasn't ready to come to the net. Once more, I trudged back to the car, certain that Tom would lose the fish during my journey. Nevertheless, he was still struggling with the big fish when I returned. About five minutes later he landed it using the long-handled pike net.

We admired the 15-pound fish and returned it to the river. It was the first steelhead any of us had ever caught. Later, casting a single-hooked spoon upstream and retrieving it along the bottom, a method which I later learned was illegal because it was being misused to snag steelhead, I caught one that went around four pounds. I caught several more four pounders the next morning using a spawn sack in the Salmon River.

Using a nine-foot fly rod blank, I created a spin rod, later referred to as a noodle rod, for use on Lake Ontario tributaries. The long rod and sensitive tip allowed me to feel the subtle take when the steelhead engulfed the egg sack and to better play and land the fish on a four-pound tippet. Using a noodle rod, an angler set the two-pound-test tippet world freshwater record for steelhead with a 16-1/2-pound fish caught in the Salmon River in 1982. Later, I used a three-piece, ten-foot, fly rod for seven-weight lines, with a fly reel loaded with an oversized shooting head attached to a level running line, and my noodle rod has been collecting dust ever since.

Bob, who used a standard six-foot spin rod when we first fished the river, hooked over a half a dozen steelhead at the head of one pool in an hour's time, but was unable to land a single one. His rod was too short and too light to put any pressure on these big fish. I tried to help by going way downstream in an effort to net the fish, but it was futile. Each big fish would surge into deeper water each time I tried to swoop it up from behind. Limbs from fallen trees hung out over the water and others dragged in the current. Stepping over and around these limbs in the fast current, while trying to net a 15-pound fish and not slip on the rocks was no easy task. And remember, the water was rising rapidly. I soon became tired. Because Bob was unable to apply enough pressure, each fish gained strength while it held in the current and then ran downstream until it reached the rapids, where the hook either straightened out, came loose, or the tippet broke.

When Bob hooked his seventh fish, I refused to try to net it, and he hasn't forgiven me since, stating, "If you think you're tired, try standing in the rising current, holding the rod high over your head, and leaning back to apply pressure on the fish."

I replied, "That's exactly what I am going to do," but, by now, the water was quite high and I didn't have a single hit.

In the early years of the steelhead runs, the fish grew big, with Tom catching several over 20 pounds on four-pound-test tippet. We were unable to weigh these fish on a certified International Game and Fish Association Scale, a requirement when a fish is submitted to the association for confirmation, so Tom doesn't hold the four-pound-test tippet record for his fish, but unlike some anglers, he doesn't really care. A Glover, Vermont angler reported catching a state-record rainbow close to 14 pounds in the Black Creek. After pressure from those who knew the river, he admitted that the fish had been raised in a pond and brought to the creek.

One February, Tom and I drove the four hours from our home to the Salmon to try for late-running steelhead. Water was not being released from the dam, but a steady stream of water was coming over the top, keeping the river at a depth where we could fish it all day long. After breaking up the ice along the shore, I waded into a likely spot below a run and began short-sticking a spawn sack upstream. Every two minutes or so, I would have to stick my whole rod down into the water to melt the ice that formed on the guides. Gloves with the fingertips cut off weren't working out either and my hands were freezing.

After a short time, two guys came up the river and stopped opposite me on the opposite bank. They watched me for a while and then rigged up. The first to enter the water tossed his sack up into the same run I was fishing and was immediately into a bright silver fish. When he followed the fish downstream, his companion entered the river at the same spot and tossed his sack up into the run. Like his friend, he immediately hooked another strong fish and took off downstream after it. The first guy passed him on the way up and they both exclaimed, "Isn't this great!" When he returned to his spot directly across from me he bellowed, "This is the first time we've fished for steelhead! How are you doing?"

The other side of the river phenomena reared its ugly head again. And if that wasn't enough, shortly thereafter, I fell in the water (which was a lot warmer than the air), and, as I stripped off layers of my wet clothing, each piece froze stiff in the 15°F temperature. I ran back to the car nude, carrying my cardboard cloths, with Tom laughing at me from upstream. Shivering, I put on a new set of clothes and vowed never to do this again. After all, wasn't fishing a spring and summer sport? Why was I doing it in the dead of winter? It was on this trip that I decided to take up skiing and leave winter fishing to others.

After I settled down, however, I realized that winter fishing has its own unique charm. At first, the winter landscape seemed to be one bleak color — gray. But after a while, I began to appreciate the subtle differences, like the misty blue haze that hung over a feeder stream. Walking along the riverbank, I saw an old oak standing guard over a flock of younger trees, bearing the brunt of the cold winds and heavy snows. I spotted a cardinal perched in an evergreen, making the snow look even whiter. Pausing on my backcast, I looked up into the sky and saw jets drawing lines across the horizon. On my next cast, the lines were scattered by the winds.

When I left the river in the evening, orange and purple streaked the sky and slithered down to glowing embers along the horizon. The snowy winter evening woods were quiet — like a woolen comforter had been placed over the land to muffle the sound. When we arrived back at our car, the sky was a deeper blue than when we first arrived and the first stars began to shine brightly. A short time later, the sky glittered with stars and I paused to wonder if we are really alone in this endless universe. Once more, I felt glad to be alive. And when I left the river for home, I made plans to come again when a break in the weather got my juices flowing.

## The Arrival of the Drift Boat

Eventually drift boats appeared on the river and their captains held these boats just above a good hole and instructed their clients to drift deep-running lures or bait into the holes. Bob and I hired a guide and took a drift boat trip, mostly to see the whole river in case there were spots we hadn't discovered when walking in from side roads. I hooked a 12-pounder, but I was so cold that fighting the fish made me shake all over. Even when the fish tired, it was difficult to pull it upstream through the strong current. I don't know which fought harder the fish or the current!

When the drift boat guides learned to fish the river, the real economic boom began. Now anglers could fish the Salmon River when it was swollen. Now wealthy sportsmen were attracted to the river. A private section of the Salmon, just above the mouth, opened as a fish-for-a-fee section. The few small sporting good stores in Pulaski expanded, and half-a-dozen more sprang up. New motels and fishing lodges appeared and the economically depressed area was now no longer depressed. Later, fly-fishing-only sections were established on the Salmon River above Altmar.

We never fished for the football-shaped browns that moved into the lower river shortly after the salmon run, although we caught some in the lake from Tom's boat. The majority have never been in the river, having been transferred to the Salmon River Hatchery from other hatcheries as fingerlings, raised at Altmar until about 14 months of age, and then released into the river at its mouth. Consequently, the majority of browns are caught downstream from Pulaski in the Douglaston pay-to-fish section. The current world-record brown trout in the two-pound-tippet line class is 12 1/4 pounds, caught in Grindstone Creek, another tributary to Lake Ontario.

I haven't fished the Lake Ontario tributaries much since our initial surge of interest in the early 1980s. Tom still goes regularly and he catches fish, but none over 15 pounds. He now uses a fly rod, tossing flies tied with ice chenille bodies and action yarn tails, glow bugs, or stonefly nymphs. An agreement between DEC and the power company has resulted in small, steady releases throughout the day and night.

Consequently, Tom fishes all day, unless it becomes too cold for his taste. Because of the stable releases, stoneflies are reestablishing themselves in the river, flies whose eggs hatch in the winter and, therefore, become a food source for migrating steelhead. The tiny winter black stonefly is imitated with a size 16 nymph and the early black and early brown stoneflies imitated with a size 10 nymph. Because the consistent releases have resulted in the return of streamborn flies, trout may be stocked in the river.

In more recent years, there has been a limited run of Skamania steelhead in July, making the river a year-round fishery. Since 1995, efforts also have been made to reintroduce Atlantic salmon into the river, thereby creating a more natural fishery. Whether they will survive the many "cancan" dancers along the river remains to be seen

## Getting There and Getting Started

Before a trip is planned, the Salmon River Hotline (800-452-1742, ext. 365123 [the six-digit water-line-cite code]) or the Oswego County Fish and

TOM ROYSTER

*Working for steelhead below Route 2A Bridge.*

Fun Line (800-248-4FUN), should be called to check water levels and release times. The Fish and Fun Line also gives the current weather and a seven-day weather forecast. I also use the Fish and Fun Line to get information on Mexico Bay because it tells me if the Little Sandy is running or is frozen over, a clue to whether the other small creeks can be fished.

If the releases on the Salmon are less than 500 cubic feet per second, the river is too low to fish. If at 750 cfs (the first unit of release), the river not only can be fly-fished throughout, but can be easily crossed in a number of places. When the release is much above 900 cfs, fly-fishing becomes difficult. In late March when the snow melts, and the flow per second can get to 1,500 cfs, only spin fishermen with special rigs can keep bait on the bottom. If the snow melt is accompanied by heavy rain, as so often happens in late March and early April, the flow per second can get to 2,000 cfs and the river cannot be fished. We had heavy snow falls late in the winter of 2001 and when I called on April 20, the river was running at 6,000 cfs.

If planing a summer trip, one of the sports stores, such as Whitaker's (315-298-6162), will tell the caller the water temperature. The water in the river is usually quite warm in the summer, putting considerable stress on the

Skamania steelhead. If the water temperature is less than 65°, then a trip may result in your landing fish up to 20 pounds. Fish with a heavy tippet so fish can be landed quickly. Keep them in the water while removing the hook, and make sure a fish has been revived before you let it swim off. Sparsely tied flies in dark colors work best, but several different sizes may need to be tried before you find the size fish like best.

If the water temperature is above 65° in the river when you get there, the estuaries of Lake Ontario offer excellent largemouth bass and northern pike fishing. Canoes, boats, and float tubes can also be used to stalk these fish, while your family either fishes with you or swims in the crystal-clear lake water at one of the nearby beaches. A boat can be rented at one of the marinas to fish for large smallmouth in the lake's bays and coves. Early morning or late afternoon fishing in the shallow water near drop-offs will usually produce fish.

From Syracuse, Pulaski is reached by driving north on U.S. 81 and taking the Pulaski exit. Most of the motels are located near the exit, as is Whitaker's Sports Shop, one of the first full-service shops in the area. All Seasons Sport, Tony's Country Sport, and Yankee Fly and Tackle are located in the village and the Fish Inn Post and Melinda's Fly and Tackle are located upstream at Altmar. All these shops sell river maps and make arrangements for guide services.

The first of the two catch-and-release fly-fishing sections starts at the County Road Bridge at Altmar, where there is a large parking lot, and it extends to a marked boundary less than a quarter-of-a-mile upstream at Beaverdam Brook. The season runs from September 15 to May 15. The second section starts on the upstream side of the Salmon River Fish Hatchery and goes upstream to the Lighthouse Hill Reservoir. The season is from April 1 to November 30. Weighted flies, with a hook gap no greater than half an inch are permitted. The leader cannot be longer than 15 feet and extra weights can be placed no more than four feet above the fly. Unlike in fall, the river is not crowded in the winter so a trip to the fly-fishing-only section is usually unnecessary. If fishing for salmon, then the sections are worth a visit.

The Douglaston Salmon Run, one of two pay-to-fish sections on the river, is thought to be affordable by most. Located west of Pulaski, it is off Route 5 which runs into Route 3, at the lake. It is a good spot if you hope to encounter the big browns running up from the lake towards the end of the salmon run. The Barkley Run is a famous run in this section, as is Josh Hole, a deep pool bounded on one side by an island and on the other by a rock cliff. The town now charges a small fee to fish the Black Hole, so the team of fly-fishermen I spoke of earlier has either retired or relocated to another spot.

## Accommodations and Other Activities

I know of no other area that has experienced such rapid growth in motels and lodges. When the state started to stock anadromous fish in Lake Ontario in 1981, primarily to stimulate a depressed economy, there were only several motels in the area. Now there are numerous motels and lodges in Pulaski, Altmar, and Sandy Creek. Our group has stayed at Whitaker's Sports Store and Lodge (315-298-3162) and the Redwood Motel (315-298-4717) and, more recently, Tom has stayed at the Pulaski Super 8 Motel, all located at the Pulaski exit of Highway 81.

There are number of fishing lodges located right on the river that were acquired when property values skyrocketed and residents sold their riverfront homes to make a killing, or else converted them into fishing lodges. Each time we visited the river, another lodge appeared along its banks. One of them, The Lodge (315-298-6672), is located on the Douglaston Salmon Run and another, the Fish Post Inn (315-298-6406), is located 50 yards from the fly-fishing-only section at Altmar. For a complete listing of motels and lodges, anglers can call the Fish-N-Fun line or visit the Oswego County web site at www.co.oswego.ny.us.

If you pick up a guide book, even the *Mobile Travel Guide*, Pulaski is not listed in the index. Pulaski does have a fine arts center, a historical society, and the Fernwood Hydro Processing Facility, where, at a restored feed mill, visitors can watch one of the few remaining restored water turbines in action. Nevertheless, I would not recommend bringing your family to Pulaski, unless, of course, they are all fisherpersons, nor should you bring a partner who needs your constant company. If you visit the Salmon in the early fall, both the West and East Canada creeks, a short distance north of the New York Turnpike, above Herkimer, offer acceptable brown trout fishing.